★

BENJAMIN BRITTEN

A Sketch of his Life and Works

★

By the same author

STRAVINSKY'S SACRIFICE TO APOLLO, 1930

WALKING SHADOWS: an essay on Lotte Reiniger's
Silhouette Films, 1931

THE LITTLE CHIMNEY SWEEP, 1936

STRAVINSKY: a critical survey, 1947

THE RISE OF ENGLISH OPERA, 1951

BENJAMIN BRITTEN

ERIC WALTER WHITE

*

BENJAMIN BRITTEN

A Sketch of his Life and Works

*

new edition
revised and enlarged

BOOSEY & HAWKES Limited

London · Paris · Bonn · Capetown · Sydney · Toronto · New York

Printed in Great Britain

To

Bettina Hürlimann-Kiepenheuer

PREFACE

to the second edition

Early in 1946 I was invited by Atlantis Verlag of Zurich to write a monograph on Benjamin Britten for inclusion in their special series, Atlantis-Musikbücherei. Impressed by this evidence of foreign interest in a contemporary British composer and by the initiative shown by a foreign publishing house in commissioning the first book to appear in any country on Britten and his music, I accepted their offer with pleasure. *Benjamin Britten: eine Skizze von Leben und Werk* accordingly appeared in November 1948 in a German translation by Bettina and Martin Hürlimann, and the English edition was published a few days later by Boosey & Hawkes, Ltd.

In the Preface to that edition I wrote: 'The special significance of Britten as a composer is that in an age when there is a perilous tendency for the artist to become divorced from society, he has succeeded to an unique extent in bridging that gap. The best of his music meets with the approval, not only of the connoisseur, but also of the general public. This can be most clearly seen in his operas and in many of his choral and vocal works.'

The works he has composed during the last five years have fully confirmed my views. Believing him to be one of the most important opera composers of the twentieth century, I have had no hesitation in giving special prominence to his operas in this book; and I am glad that the issue of this second edition has given me an opportunity, not only to revise the text of the chapters on *Peter Grimes*, *The Rape of Lucretia* and *Albert Herring*, but also to include new chapters on *Paul Bunyan*, *The Beggar's Opera*, *The Little Sweep*, *Billy Budd* and *Gloriana*.

The bibliography and list of gramophone recordings have been dropped in view of the comprehensive treatment given to these matters in *Benjamin Britten: a commentary on his works by a group of specialists* edited by Donald Mitchell and Hans Keller (Rockliff, 1952). But there is a new appendix giving details of the productions of Britten's operas at home and abroad, set out in the same way as the material in Alfred Loewenberg's authoritative *Annals of Opera* (Heffer, 1943); and an index has been added.

Acknowledgments are due to a number of persons, particularly W. H. Auden, for permission to quote from copyright material.

I wish to thank all those who have generously supplied me with information—especially Henry Boys, Eric Crozier, Iris Lemare, Elisabeth Mayer, Erwin Stein and Basil Wright—and also Hilda Montgomery who helped to prepare this book for the press. To Britten himself I owe a great debt for his unfailing kindness and help. But though he has seen the text and commented on it in draft, the final responsibility for the present book is mine alone.

E. W. W.

London, August 1953

CONTENTS

x CONTENTS

PART ONE

Life and Environment

CHAPTER I

Early Works and Training

Edward Benjamin Britten was born at Lowestoft, Suffolk, on St. Cecilia's Day (November 22) 1913, the youngest of four children. His father was a dental surgeon, and his mother a keen amateur singer, who acted for some years as secretary of the Lowestoft Choral Society. The Britten family lived in a house directly facing the North Sea.

Music was an early love of his. He started to compose at the age of five. Piano lessons began when he was seven, and viola lessons when he was ten or eleven. There were other activities too. Some years later when he was accorded the freedom of his home town, he recalled his appearance on the stage of The Sparrow's Nest as 'a very small boy, dressed in skin-coloured tights, with madly curly hair, trying desperately to remember the lines spoken by Tom the water-baby, sitting on the lap of Mrs. Do-as-you-would-be-done-by'[1] played on this occasion by his mother. It is appropriate that this musician should have shown so early an interest in the stage.

His activity as a juvenile composer was phenomenal. He himself has described these early efforts as follows:[2] 'I remember the first time I tried, the result looked rather like the Forth Bridge, in other words hundreds of dots all over the page connected by long lines all joined together in beautiful curves. I am afraid it was the pattern on the paper which I was interested in and when I asked my mother to play it, her look of horror upset me considerably. My next efforts were much more conscious of *sound*. I had started playing the piano and wrote elaborate tone poems usually lasting about twenty seconds, inspired by terrific events in

---

[1]From Benjamin Britten's speech at Lowestoft, July 28, 1951.

[2]From *The Composer and the Listener*, a broadcast talk by Benjamin Britten, November 7, 1946.

my home life such as the departure of my father for London, the appearance in my life of a new girl friend or even a wreck at sea. My later efforts luckily got away from these emotional inspirations and I began to write sonatas and quartets which were not connected in any direct way with life. . . . At school I somehow managed to be able to fit in a great deal of writing with the extremely busy life that everyone leads at school. . . . I wrote symphony after symphony, song after song, a tone poem called *Chaos and Cosmos*, although I fear I was not sure what these terms really meant.' By the time he left his preparatory school, South Lodge, at the age of fourteen to enter Gresham's School, Holt, he had already written ten piano sonatas, six string quartets, three suites for piano, an oratorio, and dozens of songs. Some of this piano music and three of the songs were arranged later for string orchestra in the *Simple Symphony* (1934). Most of the unpublished early compositions are still extant and, if the composer ever agreed to make them accessible, would provide interesting material for a study in musical precocity.

In 1926 Audrey Alston, his viola teacher in Norwich, introduced him to the composer, Frank Bridge, who, feeling certain that his juvenile outpourings revealed signs of a talent of unusual musical promise, arranged to give him special tuition in harmony and counterpoint during the school holidays. This discipline was especially salutary to a person of Britten's facility and fluency. Prolonged study and hard work were the order of the day; but Bridge knew how to temper his criticism so that, however stern it may have been, it never had the effect of discouraging his young and enthusiastic pupil.

After two years at Gresham's School, Holt (from September 1928 to July 1930), Britten won a Composition Scholarship to the Royal College of Music, London. His examiners on that occasion were John Ireland, S. P. Wad-

dington and Ralph Vaughan Williams. During the next
three years he worked under John Ireland for composition
and Arthur Benjamin for piano. He won the Ernest Farrar
Prize for composition and passed the examination for the
Associateship of the College as a solo pianist in 1933.

Although some of his works now began to be published
and performed, many still remained unheard. For instance, M. Montagu-Nathan, when acting as secretary of
the Camargo Society in 1932, met Britten at a party and,
finding this young student had written a ballet score, pre-
vailed on him to submit it. Whether the manuscript was
ever read by Edwin Evans, the Society's Chairman, or
Constant Lambert, its conductor, is not known; but in the
course of time the score was returned to the composer and
nothing more was heard of it.[1]

But there is no doubt that the importance of Britten's
period as a student resided less in the quantity and quality
of his compositions than in the fact that he now had better
opportunities for hearing music, especially contemporary
music, making friends with other musicians and generally
broadening his intellectual horizon. Among the classics, the
strongest influences on his work were Mozart and Schubert,
rather than Beethoven and Brahms. (His love of Purcell
was a later growth.) His feeling for melody and lyricism led
him to find in Mahler a congenial spirit. He was convinced
that in compositions like *Des Knaben Wunderhorn* and the
Kindertotenlieder, Mahler had expressed the idea behind
the music with such success as to achieve real perfection of
musical form. Among contemporary composers, he particularly admired the works of Strawinsky, Schönberg and
Berg. He tried (in vain) to get the score of *Pierrot Lunaire*
bought for the library at the College. In the autumn of 1934
he visited Vienna; but, to his great disappointment, his

---

[1]'A Lost Opportunity' by M. Montagu-Nathan. *Radio Times*, July 31,
1953.

parents, acting on the advice of the College authorities, did not allow him to study with Berg. However, he attended the broadcast concert performance of *Wozzeck* at the Queen's Hall on March 14, 1934, and although in the concert hall this opera naturally lacked the extraordinary effectiveness of its stage presentation, the impact it made was still overwhelming.

It was outside rather than inside the College[1] that Britten found opportunities for the performance of his early compositions; and it was at the MacNaghton-Lemare concerts of new music given at the Ballet Club Theatre (later known as the Mercury Theatre) that the public first heard his music. A *Phantasy for String Quintet* in one movement (unpublished) and Three Two-Part Songs for female voices to words by Walter de la Mare were given at the concert on December 12, 1932; and the performance was noticed by *The Times*, *The Musical Times* and *Music Lover*.[2]

On January 31, 1933, came the *Sinfonietta* for chamber orchestra which had been written the previous summer;

---

[1] The only work of his to be performed at the Royal College of Music was the *Sinfonietta* (op. 1) which was included in the programme of the chamber concert on March 16, 1933.

[2] It was in *Music Lover* that 'C.D.' praised the three part songs as being 'good from one who, I believe, is only 19; even though they were reminiscent in a quite peculiar degree of Walton's latest songs which were heard recently elsewhere'. The Walton songs referred to were the Three Songs from *Façade* which had been performed for the first time at the Wigmore Hall on October 10, 1932. That this inapposite comment riled the composer can be seen from the opening of his article 'Variations on a Critical Theme' printed in *Opera*, March 1952. 'I can well remember my first contact with the critics. I was about 17 and three part songs of mine had been given at a London theatre concert. They were written as a student's exercise, with the voice parts in strict canon. The first was amiably grotesque, the second atmospheric in a cool way, the third lumpily "folky". The only written criticism of this performance damned them entirely—as being obvious copies of Walton's three Façade Songs. Now anyone who is interested can see for himself that this is silly nonsense. The Walton Songs are brilliant and sophisticated in the extreme—mine could scarcely have been more childlike and naive, with not a trace of parody throughout. It is easy to imagine the damping effect of this first notice on a young composer. I was furious and dismayed because I could see there was not a word of truth in it. I was also considerably discouraged.'

and the programme of the concert on December 11, 1933, included Two Part-Songs for Mixed Choir and another unpublished work, entitled *Alla Quartetto Serioso*—'*Go play, boy, play*'. A programme note stated: 'This Quartet is not yet finished. There will be five movements in all, the three movements that are ready being the first, second, and fifth,' viz. 1. Alla Marcia, 2. Alla Valse (the dance), 5. Alla Burlesca (ragging).

In 1934, the year in which Holst, Delius and Elgar died, Britten came of age. He had left the College the previous December and was starting the difficult business of earning his living by composing. In addition to the works mentioned above, he had already written the *Phantasy Quartet* for oboe, violin, viola and cello, and a set of choral variations for mixed voices unaccompanied entitled *A Boy was Born*; and during the year he was to add the *Simple Symphony*, and also a collection of twelve children's songs for voice and piano, *Friday Afternoons*, a piano suite entitled *Holiday Diary*, and a suite for violin and piano. None of these works had long to wait for performance. The *Phantasy Quartet* was first played by Leon Goossens and the International String Quartet in London and also at the 1934 I.S.C.M. Festival at Florence. *A Boy was Born* was broadcast by the B.B.C. on February 23, 1934; and when it was given its first public performance at the MacNaghton-Lemare concert of December 17, 1934, it received a glowing review from A. H. Fox-Strangways in *The Observer*.[1] '[The music] has one mark of mastery' he wrote, 'endless invention and facility. [The composer] takes what he wants, and does not trouble about what other people have thought well to take. He rivets attention from the first note onwards: without knowing in the least what is coming, one feels instinctively that this is music it behoves one to listen to and each successive moment strengthens that feeling.'

[1] Afterwards reprinted in *Music Observed*, Methuen, 1936.

Not all the critics were as enthusiastic as Fox-Strangways. On several occasions 'J.A.W.' complained in *The Daily Telegraph* that 'the solving of technical problems' seemed to 'occupy the composer's mind to the exclusion of musical ideas'; and William McNaught wrote: 'This young spark is good company for as long as his persiflage remains fresh, which is not very long. To do him justice, his *Sinfonietta* closed down in good time.'

The need to earn money by composition led him to turn to the cinema. Fortunately this was the period when John Grierson had collected some remarkably talented persons to work on documentary films for the G.P.O. Film Unit; and Britten joined the group in 1935. In the five years 1935–39 he produced incidental music for sixteen documentary films by the G.P.O. Film Unit, two documentary films by other units, and one feature film, *Love from a Stranger* (Trafalgar Films), directed by Rowland V. Lee.

He entered into this work with great zest and seems to have enjoyed its special conditions and restrictions. Some years later, when recalling this period of his life, he said[1]: 'I had to work quickly, to force myself to work when I didn't want to and to get used to working in all kinds of circumstances. The film company I was working for was not a big commercial one, it was a documentary company and had very little money. I had to write scores not for large orchestras but for six or seven instruments, and to make these instruments make all the effects that each film demanded. I also had to be very ingenious and try to imitate, not necessarily by musical instruments, but in the studio, the natural sounds of every-day life. I well remember the mess we made in the studio one day when trying to fit an appropriate sound to shots of a large ship unloading in a dock. We had pails of water which we slopped everywhere, drain pipes with coal slipping down them, model

---

[1]From *The Composer and the Listener*, op. cit.

railways, whistles and every kind of paraphernalia we could think of.' In a short time he built up a considerable reputation in this specialized field. In 1936, shortly after the release of *Coal Face*, a pictorial survey of the coal industry in Great Britain, directed by Grierson with music by Britten, Kurt London wrote[1]: 'It is astonishing to observe how, with the most scanty material, using only a piano and a speaking chorus, he can make us dispense gladly with realistic sounds. This stylization makes a much stronger impression than a normal musical accompaniment.'

As soon as it was realized that this young composer had a flair for occasional and incidental music, commissions for theatre and radio as well as further film work followed. Britten was prepared to oblige with every type of music, light or serious; and the successful undertaking of these commissions showed that he was a reliable business man, who could work quickly and to time, and make the best of the limitations of the particular medium he was writing for and of the resources (however modest) that had been placed at his disposal. These virtues have always stood him in good stead. It is now well known that he is able to complete the greater part of the composition of a new work in his head so that (as was the case with Mozart) the act of committing it to paper becomes an almost mechanical process which can be carried out at high speed. There is the added advantage that this enables him to plan his musical life in advance so that he knows with reasonable certainty when he will be free to compose and by what date he can promise delivery of a new work. Reliability, expeditiousness and an unfailing capacity for hard work: these are formidable assets for an artist to have. When they are allied to an instinctive talent of no mean order, the result is bound to be phenomenal.

---

[1] *Film Music* by Kurt London, Faber and Faber, 1936.

CHAPTER II

Collaboration with W. H. Auden

Four years before Britten entered Gresham's School, Holt, W. H. Auden, one of the older boys at the same school published his first poem, *Woods in Rain*,[1] a set of octosyllabic couplets in the conventional Georgian style. In 1926 he became one of the editors of *Oxford Poetry*; and his undergraduate poems, which had wide currency at the University, showed him at that time to be under the influence of masters like Rainer Maria Rilke and T. S. Eliot. By 1930 when his *Poems* were published by Faber and Faber, he had found his distinctive style.

Poems has rightly been hailed as a landmark of modern poetry. It is also a prophetic book, alive with a premonition of the doom that was so soon to bring disaster to the world. These thirty poems are imbued with a sense of struggle: war between classes, between parties, between members— war between life and death. But there is never any doubt what action has to be taken:

> *. . . never serious misgiving*
> *Occurred to anyone,*
> *Since there could be no question of living*
> *If we did not win.*[2]

In fact, more important still, the danger is seen to be actual not potential, and the poet analyses the new technique of total warfare with uncanny skill.

> *This is the dragon's day, the devourer's;*
> *Orders are given to the enemy for a time*
> *With underground proliferation of mould,*
> *With constant whisper and the casual question,*
> *To haunt the poisoned in his shunned house,*

---

[1] Published in *Public School Verse* Vol. IV 1923–24 (Heinemann) where the author's name was misprinted 'W. H. Arden'.

[2] *Poems* XII.

> *To destroy the efflorescence of the flesh,*
> *The intricate play of the mind, to enforce*
> *Conformity with the orthodox bone,*
> *With organized fear, the articulated skeleton.*[1]

The political awareness of Auden and of several of his contemporary poet friends, including Cecil Day Lewis, Louis MacNeice and Stephen Spender, was directed during the next few years to the struggle against Fascism in its various manifestations; and their attention was naturally focussed on the battleground in Spain, for (as Auden wrote)

> *... the time is short, and*
> *History to the defeated*
> *May say Alas but cannot help nor pardon.*[2]

Auden was not content, however, merely to write and publish poems. He looked towards stage and screen as being possibly more persuasive pulpits than the printed page. Remembering the didactic force of Bertolt Brecht's 'epic' drama, examples of which (like *Die Dreigroschenoper* and *Mahagonny*) he had seen performed in Germany at the beginning of the 'thirties, he began to experiment with social and political charades of his own, cast in the form of verse masques or plays. In *The Dance of Death*, which was published in 1933 and produced two years later by the Group Theatre at the Westminster Theatre, London, he aimed at presenting 'a picture of the decline of a class, of how its members dream of a new life, but secretly desire the old, for there is death in them'. In 1935 he wrote his first full-length verse play, *The Dog beneath the Skin, or Where is Francis?* in collaboration with Christopher Isherwood. As its alternative title implies, it is a quest drama—a search for an heir—and it was produced by the Group Theatre at the Westminster Theatre in January 1936.

---

[1] *Poems* XVI.
[2] From *Spain*, 1937, reprinted in *Another Time*, Faber and Faber, 1940.

Meanwhile, his desire to work for the cinema had led him to approach the G.P.O. Film Unit and ask his friend Basil Wright whether there was any way he could be employed in documentary films. Grierson was delighted to enlist his help; and he was forthwith engaged to write scripts for two films, *Coal Face* and *Night Mail*, that the Unit had in production. As Britten had been commissioned to provide the music for both films, it was necessary to arrange a meeting between the two collaborators. This took place on July 4, 1935, when Basil Wright drove Britten down to Colwall, near Malvern, where Auden was working as master at a boys' preparatory school called 'The Downs'.

'*Coal Face*' (wrote Basil Wright[1]) 'was a pure experiment with the sound track. Its success as a film was not great, but without it the big success of *Night Mail* could not have been achieved. In *Coal Face* (which was devised and made by Cavalcanti), Auden and Britten used for the first time the spoken voice reciting from official reports of mine disasters and from lists of coal-mining job-names—in rhythm, sometimes unaccompanied, and sometimes with percussion. *Coal Face* also contained the first musical setting by Britten of words by Auden: the poem beginning "*Oh lurcher-loving collier, black as night*" which was specially written for the film and set for female voices.' For *Night Mail*, Britten wrote a special instrumental score; and Basil Wright recalls how when 'the closing music of the film turned out to be too long, he made some fantastically ingenious excisions from the sound track itself'. After *Night Mail*, there was some talk of another film with which Auden and Britten were to be jointly concerned—an elaborate experiment about the negro in Western Civilization—but in the end this was abandoned. The only other film they were engaged on together was *The Way to the Sea* (Strand Film Company, 1937), which described the elec-

---

[1] From a letter to E. W. White dated April 1, 1948.

trification of the Portsmouth railway line, and for which Auden wrote a special commentary.

This collaboration, so auspiciously begun, soon developed outside the film world. In 1936 Britten was invited to compose a work for the Norwich and Norfolk Triennial Festival and asked Auden to devise a libretto. Auden chose man's relations to animals as his subject, selecting three poems to illustrate animals as pests, pets and prey— the first an anonymous prayer for deliverance from rats, the second an anonymous dirge on the death of a monkey entitled *Messalina*, the third *Hawking for the Partridge* by T. Ravenscroft—and framed them with an original prologue and epilogue of his own. The title of this symphonic cycle for high voice and orchestra was derived from the opening of the epilogue[1]:

> *Our hunting fathers told the story*
> *Of the sadness of the creatures,*
> *Pitied the limits and the lack*
> *Set in their finished features ...*

Auden did not completely succeed in disciplining his material, and Britten cannot have had an easy task to set it. The result was in places a satirical, poignant and savage score. According to Scott Goddard,[2] *Our Hunting Fathers* on its first performance at Norwich on September 25, 1936, 'amused the sophisticated, scandalized those among the gentry who caught Auden's words, and left musicians dazzled at so much talent, uneasy that it should be expended on so arid a subject, not knowing whether to consider Britten's daring style as the outcome of courage or foolhardiness'.

Two further verse plays came from the collaboration of Auden with Isherwood. The Group Theatre produced *The Ascent of F.6* at the Mercury Theatre, London, on Feb-

---

[1]Reprinted in *Look, Stranger!* by W. H. Auden, 1936.

[2]From *British Music of Our Time*, edited by A. L. Bacharach, Pelican Books, 1946.

ruary 26, 1937, and *On the Frontier* at the Arts Theatre, Cambridge, on November 14, 1938. To both of these Britten wrote incidental music scored for piano (four hands) and percussion; and in the case of *On the Frontier* he added parts for two trumpets. Other Group Theatre productions at the Westminster Theatre for which Britten provided music, were *Timon of Athens* (November 1935), the *Agamemnon* of Æschylus in Louis MacNeice's translation (November 1936), and MacNeice's verse play *Out of the Picture* (December 1937).

In 1937 came the first of Britten's song cycles, *On This Island.* For this he chose five lyrics by Auden, of which four came from *Look, Stranger!* and the fifth (Nocturne) was extracted from *The Dog beneath the Skin.* This selection was to have been the first of two or more volumes with the common title *On This Island:* but in the event only the first set was completed. Here Britten probably showed sound judgment, for the specific gravity of these lyrics written by Auden *dans l'an trentième de son age*, with their mixture of romance, neurosis and satire, do not call for treatment on too extended a scale. When it first appeared, *On This Island* had an exciting quality of contemporaneity—it was the product of two young minds thinking along related lines and working to a common purpose—and although it has subsequently been rather overshadowed by the later song-cycles, it is never likely to lose its special attraction.

In 1938 the collaboration was interrupted by a journey Auden and Isherwood made to the Far East to report on the Sino-Japanese War; and the only other work by Britten and Auden belonging to this year was *Hadrian's Wall*, a B.B.C. radio feature.

After Auden's return from China and the production of *On the Frontier*, there was a further occasion when they worked together. A Festival of Music for the People was organized in London 'by musicians of the progressive

movement in Britain'; and for its third concert at the
Queen's Hall on April 5, 1939, Britten wrote a *Ballad of
Heroes* to honour men of the British Battalion, International Brigade, who had fallen in Spain. This consisted
of three movements: 1. Funeral March with words by
Randall Swingler, 2. Scherzo (Dance of Death) with words
by Auden,[1] and 3. Recitative and Choral with words by
both Auden and Swingler. The moral of the work was contained in the Epilogue (Funeral March):

> *To you we speak, you numberless Englishmen,*
> *To remind you of the greatness still among you*
> *Created by these men who go from your towns*
> *To fight for peace, for liberty and for you.*

Britten set the text for tenor (or soprano) solo, chorus and
orchestra, with three extra trumpets to be played in a
gallery and (later) off; and it was conducted on this
occasion by Constant Lambert. Not unnaturally the work
is pervaded by a feeling of deep bitterness, for at that
moment the Spanish Civil War was over, and it seemed as
if the forces of reaction had triumphed everywhere.

There is no doubt that this friendship with Auden had a
great effect on Britten. It confirmed his liking for occasional
quips and quiddities. It introduced him to Auden's favourite death fixation—the obsession that the illness and death
of an individual symbolizes the decay and dissolution of a
class—and for a period he seemed to have adopted it so
wholeheartedly that it became almost a rule for his more
extended compositions to include a key movement entitled
Dance of Death or Funeral March. Fortunately, however,
he outgrew this idea before it had time to shrivel into a
fixed and meaningless *cliché*. But his most valuable and

---

[1]The poem 'It's farewell to the drawing-room's civilized cry' from which
these stanzas are taken, was first printed in *The Listener*, February 17, 1937,
under the title 'Song for the New Year', and reprinted in *Another Time*,
1940.

lasting gains were probably a fuller sense of an artist's political responsibility, a deeper appreciation of the beauties of English poetry, and a growing awareness of the esthetic problems involved in the alliance of words and music.

CHAPTER III

American Visit

Important though Britten's collaboration with Auden undoubtedly was, it would be wrong to imply that it occupied his working life during the last years of the 'thirties to the exclusion of other activities. During this period a number of other works were written and performed. In London the Lemare Concerts at the Mercury Theatre continued to feature his music. The *Te Deum* written specially for Maurice Vinden and the Choir of St. Mark's, North Audley Street, London, was performed at the Mercury Theatre on January 27, 1936, and provoked a rather curious review from Constant Lambert, who wrote in *The Sunday Referee:* 'Mr. Britten is, I admit, rather a problem to me. One cannot but admire his extremely mature and economical methods, yet the rather drab and penitential content of his music leaves me quite unmoved. At the same time he is the most outstanding talent of his generation and I would always go to hear any first performance of his.' The Suite for Violin and Piano which had been played by Antonio Brosa and Britten himself at the I.S.C.M. Festival at Barcelona in 1936, was announced for performance at the Lemare Concert of February 1, 1937, but withdrawn on account of his mother's death. (His father had died a few years previously.)

In 1937 he obtained his first big popular success with the *Variations on a Theme of Frank Bridge*. He accepted an invitation in May of that year to write a new work for the Boyd Neel String Orchestra to play at the Salzburg Festival on August 27; and Boyd Neel recalls[1] that in ten days' time he appeared 'with the complete work sketched out. In

---

[1]'The String Orchestra' by Boyd Neel in *Benjamin Britten: a commentary* (edited by Mitchell and Keller).

another four weeks it was fully scored for strings as it stands today, but for the addition of one bar'. The theme he chose came from the second of Frank Bridge's *Three Idylls* for string quartet (1911), and he wrote ten variations on it, including a March, Romance, Aria Italiana, Bourrée Classique, Wiener Walzer, Moto Perpetuo, Funeral March, Chant, and Fugue and Finale, which reveal to the full his resource and skill in dealing with a string orchestra. When some years later he was cross-examined about his preference for this medium, he replied[1]: 'I am attracted by the many features of the strings. For instance, the possibilities of elaborate *divisi*—the effect of many voices of the same kind. There is also the infinite variety of colour—the use of mutes, pizzicato, harmonics and so forth. Then again, there is the great dexterity in technique of string players. Generally speaking, I like to think of the smaller combinations of players, and I deplore the tendency of present-day audiences to expect only the luscious "tutti" effect from an orchestra.'

The work caused a sensation at Salzburg and soon gained its composer an international reputation. Within less than two years it had been played more than fifty times in various parts of Europe and America.

Late in 1937 he acquired a converted windmill at Snape in Suffolk, a few miles inland from Aldeburgh, and the first works he composed there were *Mont Juic* and the Piano Concerto.

Mont Juic, a suite of four Catalan dances for orchestra, was written in collaboration with Lennox Berkeley, who has left it on record that 'a similar approach to the problem of composition made such an association possible, and though, after agreeing upon the general shape of the movements, we worked at the different parts more or less in-

---

[1]'Conversation with Benjamin Britten.' *Tempo*, February 1944.

dependently, I hope I may claim that a reasonably homogeneous Suite emerged'.[1]

The Piano Concerto in D major was first performed at a Promenade Concert at the Queen's Hall on August 18, 1938, with the composer as soloist. In its original form, it comprised four movements: I. Toccata, II. Waltz, III. Recitative and Aria, IV. March. Britten himself explained that the work 'was conceived with the idea of exploiting the various important characteristics of the piano, such as its enormous compass, its percussive quality, and its suitability for figuration; so that it is not by any means a symphony with piano, but rather a *bravura* concerto with orchestral accompaniment'. The Toccata was undoubtedly the movement in which his intentions were most successfully carried out. Eight years later, the third movement, which had given the impression of being a weak and rhetorical setting of an imaginary script, was withdrawn and an Impromptu (or, more accurately, an air with seven variations) substituted for it.

The autumn of 1938 was overshadowed by the meeting of Hitler, Mussolini and Chamberlain at Munich. The part-song for unaccompanied mixed chorus, *Advance Democracy*, belongs to this sombre period. It was followed by the *Ballad of Heroes* mentioned in the previous chapter. And these, together with the incidental music for J. B. Priestley's *Johnson Over Jordan* (New Theatre, London, February 22, 1939), were the last works Britten wrote before leaving England for America.

It was naturally a time of great depression and unrest. Rather than become helpless victims of a new Fascist or Nazi order with its attendant persecution and misery, many persons were looking for salvation to the New World and considering the possibility of emigration. A lead in this

---

[1]'The Light Music' by Lennox Berkeley in *Benjamin Britten: a commentary* (edited by Mitchell and Keller).

direction was given by Auden. He and Isherwood visited
America early in 1939, and by the outbreak of war he had
decided that only in the United States could he find the
complete anonymity he needed if he was to break away
from the European literary family and let his individual
genius develop in full independence. Louis MacNeice
quotes him as saying that 'an artist ought either to live
where he has live roots or where he has no roots at all; that
in England today the artist feels essentially lonely, twisted
in dying roots, always in opposition to a group'.[1]

There were a number of reasons that led Britten also to
leave England in the early summer of 1939. The darkening
political situation was one. Then he was dissatisfied with
the reception of his work in this country and had a growing
sense of frustration as an artist, which he felt might be dis-
sipated by a change of scene. But the dominant factor was
certainly Auden's personal example and his decision to
become a citizen of the United States; and when Britten
first reached America, it was his firm intention to do like-
wise.

Britten was accompanied on this voyage by his friend
Peter Pears, who had been a member of the B.B.C. Singers
from 1936 to 1938 and had already toured America twice
with the New English Singers. They went first to Canada
and then were invited to New York to hear the first
American performance of the *Variations on a Theme of
Frank Bridge* by the New York Philharmonic. Friends of
Peter Pears offered the hospitality of their home on Long
Island; and 'when, driving out to Amityville, Britten read
the nostalgic word, Suffolk, on the signpost, he was delighted to be again by the sea and in his native county, although
so far from home'.[2] He stayed there for the greater part of

---

[1]Letter from Louis MacNeice printed in *Horizon*, July 1940.

[2]From 'Benjamin Britten: Another Purcell', by Phoebe Douglas. *Town
and Country*, December 1947.

the next two and a half years, with the exception of a few months spent with Auden in Brooklyn early in 1940 and a visit to California in 1941.

The Violin Concerto in D minor was the first of his works to be written in America—it was finished at St. Jovite in the Province of Quebec, Canada, shortly after his arrival and received its first performance (March 27, 1940) by the New York Philharmonic under John Barbirolli, with Antonio Brosa as soloist. Although the violin part, which was edited by Brosa himself, calls for great virtuosity from its executant, the Concerto is by no means an extended violin solo with orchestral accompaniment, but represents a real advance on the Piano Concerto in powers of construction. Its final movement, a *passacaglia*, is of special interest, for it marks the first time Britten has used this particular form, which later becomes such a characteristic feature of his work. Another composition belonging to this period is *Canadian Carnival* (*Kermesse Canadienne*), a light-hearted frolic for symphony orchestra.

But more important than either of these was *Les Illuminations*, which was finished at Amityville on October 25, 1939. When this song cycle for high voice and string orchestra was first performed in London on January 30, 1940, it not only confirmed the uniformly favourable impression made by the *Variations on a Theme of Frank Bridge* two years previously, but also showed Britten to be a song-writer of exceptional range and subtlety. At the time the prose poems in *Les Illuminations* were written, Rimbaud, who was living in London with Verlaine and spending much of his time in the East End and the docks, was still arrogantly hoping that through the impetus of debauch and vice he could obtain the power of supernatural vision; and in poems like *Métropolitain*, *Villes* and *Parade* (the last two of which are included in Britten's cycle) he seemed to have discovered all the monstrous significance of a modern industrial capital. '*J'ai seul la clef de cette parade sauvage.*' Contact with the fierce alchemy of these poems quickened a new nerve in Britten's musical sensibility. The words and music fused in a sudden and startling outburst of heat and energy.

The *Diversions* for piano and orchestra were written in Maine in the summer of 1940 for the left-handed Viennese pianist, Paul Wittgenstein, who reserved the sole rights of performance until 1951. This work consisted of 'eleven straightforward and concise variations on a simple musical theme'; and in an introductory comment to the concerto, Britten said: 'I was attracted from the start by the problems involved in writing a work for this particular medium, especially as I was well acquainted with and extremely enthusiastic about Mr. Wittgenstein's skill in overcoming what appear to be insuperable difficulties. In no place in the work did I attempt to imitate a two-handed piano technique, but concentrated on exploiting and emphasizing the single line approach. I have tried to treat the problem in every aspect, as a glance at the list of movements will show: special features are trills and scales in the Recitative, widespread arpeggios in the Nocturne, agility over the keyboard in the Badinerie and Toccata, and repeated notes in the final Tarantella.' (The revised version of 1951 omits one of the variations—*Ritmico*.)

The *Sinfonia da Requiem*, written about the same time, had a particularly strange history.

Having been approached through the British Council some time in 1940 and asked whether he would write a symphony for a special festivity connected with the reigning dynasty of a foreign power, Britten agreed in principle, provided it was understood no form of musical jingoism was called for. On further investigation, it appeared that the country in question was Japan and the festivity the 2,600th anniversary of the foundation of the Mikado's dynasty in 660 B.C. by Jimmu Tenno, and that other composers in France, Germany, Italy and Hungary had received similar commissions. In due course, the outline of a *Sinfonia da Requiem* in three movements —*Lacrymosa, Dies Irae,* and *Requiem Aeternam*—was submitted to the Japanese authorities and approved. Britten felt that this work, which is permeated with a sense of the terror and ghastliness of war, would be not inappropriate to the occasion in view of the Sino-Japanese conflict. He was wrong, however; and about six months after the completed score had been handed over, he received a furious protest through the Japanese Embassy, complaining that the Christian dogma and liturgical ceremony that lay at the basis of the work were a calculated insult to the Mikado, and rejecting the *Sinfonia* out of hand. With Auden's help he drafted a suitable reply; but shortly afterwards the Japanese attacked the Americans at Pearl Harbour, and thenceforth all communications were severed. The first performance of the *Sinfonia de Requiem* was given on March 30, 1941, by the New York Philharmonic under Barbirolli. There is no record of a performance in Tokio, although it seems possible the work may have been put into rehearsal there sometime in 1941.

In the list of Britten's published works to which opus numbers have been given, two gaps occur between opus 15 (the Violin Concerto) and opus 18 (*Les Illuminations*). One of these missing opus numbers was reserved for a set of about half a dozen choral settings of poems by Gerard Manley Hopkins, which Britten withdrew from publication and performance as being not up to standard: the other for *Paul Bunyan*, which was written early in 1941. This choral operetta, in which Britten's partnership with Auden was resumed, was put on for a week's run at the Brander Matthews Hall, Columbia University, New York, in May 1941. Their treatment of this American legend came in for some hard knocks—Britten himself wrote a few years later 'the critics damned it unmercifully, but the public seemed to find something enjoyable in the performance'.[1] Neither score nor text has been published. In fact, the work was submitted to so many changes and revisions during its brief run that no definitive version can be said to exist.

Britten wrote incidental music for one or two Columbia broadcasts while he was in America; in particular, a monologue by Auden for Dame May Whitty, and *The Rocking-Horse Winner*. He also executed various ballet commissions. *Soirées Musicales*, a suite of five movements that he had adapted from Rossini in 1936 for the use of the G.P.O. Film Unit had already been used by Antony Tudor to accompany a ballet called *Soirée Musicale* that was produced by the London Ballet at the Palladium, London, on November 26, 1938. But when in 1941 Lincoln Kirstein wanted a new ballet for the South American tour of his American Ballet, Britten composed another suite after Rossini called *Matinées Musicales*, joined this to his *Soirées Musicales* suite, and added the Overture to *La Cenerentola* as a finale. The resulting ballet was called *Divertimento*, and its choreography was composed by Balanchine. About the same time Britten made a new orchestral version of *Les Sylphides* for Ballet Presentations Inc. (Ballet Theater), New York City. There was some talk of his writing a ballet for Eugene Loring and his Dance Players to be called *The Invisible Wife*; but in the end that project came to nothing. Instead, he allowed his *Variations on a Theme of Frank Bridge* to be used by Dance Players as an accompaniment to *Jinx*, a ballet about circus people and their superstitions with choreography by Lew Christensen. This was first performed in 1942 at the National Theatre, New York.

He visited Ethel and Rae Robertson in California in the summer of 1941, and during his stay at Escondido wrote

---

[1] *Peter Grimes: Sadler's Wells Opera Books No. 3.*

various two-piano compositions for them: the *Introduction and Rondo alla Burlesca*, the *Mazurka Elegiaca* in memory of Paderewski, and the *Scottish Ballad* for two pianos and orchestra. At the same time he was busy on his String Quartet No. 1, which had been commissioned by that great American patroness of music, Elizabeth Sprague Coolidge, and was performed later that summer by the Coolidge String Quartet.

But, meanwhile, what had happened to his intention of seeking naturalization as an American citizen? When the second World War broke out in September 1939, he realized that, had he still been in England, scruples of conscience would have prevented him from becoming a combatant; but he could not help wondering whether, should he decide to return, there might be ways in which his services as a non-combatant might be useful. The progress of the war aggravated his mood of indecision. Louis MacNeice, who had numerous discussions with Auden in the autumn of 1940, wrote back to war-racked England: 'For the expatriate there is no Categorical Imperative bidding him return—or stay. Auden, for example, working eight hours a day in New York, is getting somewhere; it might well be "wrong" for him to return. For another artist who felt he was getting nowhere it might be "right" to return'.[1]

In Britten's case, the mental struggle whether to stay in America or return to England was echoed by a physical illness. He suffered from an acute streptococcal infection during the whole of 1940. (It was perhaps typical of Auden that he should claim that this illness was nothing more than the physical expression of Britten's psychological indecision.) But as he recovered the following year, his course seemed crystal clear. He would not become a naturalized American, but he would go back to England. His decision to return was confirmed by a strange incident that was

[1]From 'Traveller's Return'. *Horizon*, February 1941.

destined to have important repercussions on his future career. During his stay in California he happened to pick up a copy of the B.B.C.'s weekly magazine, *The Listener*, for May 29, 1941, and there his eyes were caught by the opening words of an article by E. M. Forster: 'To think of Crabbe is to think of England.' Forster was discussing George Crabbe, the East Anglian poet of the late eighteenth and early nineteenth centuries, who had been born at Aldeburgh, not far from Lowestoft. Reading how this bleak little fishing village on the Suffolk coast 'huddles round a flint-towered church and sprawls down to the North Sea—and what a wallop the sea makes as it pounds at the shingle!' Britten realized with a twinge of homesickness that he must not only familiarize himself with Crabbe's poems (which at that time he did not know), but also get back to his native Suffolk as quickly as possible.

But it was not easy to cross the Atlantic at that stage of the war; and he and Peter Pears were kept waiting for nearly six months on the East Coast of the United States before they could obtain a passage in March 1942. The delay had certain compensations, however. It meant he was able to attend a performance of the *Sinfonia da Requiem* under Serge Koussevitsky in Boston. When in the course of conversation the conductor asked him why he had as yet written no full-scale opera, Britten, who had already been turning over in his mind the possibility of quarrying material for an opera out of Crabbe's poem *The Borough*, replied that 'the construction of a scenario, discussions with a librettist, planning the musical architecture, composing preliminary sketches, and writing nearly a thousand pages of orchestral score, demanded a freedom from other work which was an economic impossibility for most young composers'.[1] Koussevitsky was interested in the Crabbe project

---

[1] *Peter Grimes: Sadler's Wells Opera Books No. 3*, edited by Eric Crozier. The Bodley Head, 1945.

and, when they met again some weeks later, announced
that he had arranged for the Koussevitsky Music Foundation to put up $1,000 for the opera, which was to be dedi-
cated to the memory of his wife, Natalie, who had recently
died.

CHAPTER IV

In Wartime England

In the spring of 1942, the fortunes of Great Britain and her allies seemed to be at their nadir. Their disasters in Russia, the Far East and North Africa were only too apparent, and the pattern of their recovery as yet unrevealed. Nevertheless, their faith in ultimate victory was completely unshaken.

Britten returned to a land of black-out, material privations and total mobilization. In view of his conscientious objections, he was exempted from active service. He was allowed to continue with his work as a composer, and as a pianist he appeared at the special wartime concerts organized all over the country by the Council for the Encouragement of Music and the Arts (CEMA), which later grew into the Arts Council of Great Britain. Then, as always, he laid great store by his work as a musical executant. In an interview given early in 1944[1] he said : 'I find it valuable for my activities as a composer to see how listeners react to the music. I also enjoy rehearsals—especially if I am working with sympathetic and intelligent musicians—delving deeper and deeper into the great music of all ages, and learning a lot from it. There are some composers whose music I do not like, but performing it makes me analyse my reasons for the dislike, and so prevents it from becoming just habit or prejudice.'

He had left America on March 6, 1942, sailing in a small Swedish cargo boat, and by the time he reached England after being mewed up for more than a month in a tiny cabin next to the refrigerating plant, he had written two new choral works, the *Hymn to St. Cecilia* and *A Ceremony*

---

[1]'Conversation with Benjamin Britten.' *Tempo*, February 1944.

of Carols. In addition, he brought over from America a setting of *Seven Sonnets of Michelangelo* for tenor and piano, and a number of new works written and performed in the United States, but not yet heard in Great Britain. These were considerable assets. In wartime England, opportunities for hearing new music were all the more welcome because of their infrequency; and Britten's new compositions met with ready acceptance, partly because of their obviously attractive qualities of ease, grace and intelligibility, and partly also because it was immediately apparent that during his three years' residence in the United States his mind and music had strikingly matured.

Out of Michelangelo's seventy-seven sonnets, Britten chose numbers XVI, XXI, XXX, LV, XXXVIII, XXXII and XXIV—and set them in a fine flowing *bel canto* style. The pure and open vowels of the Renaissance Italian are adequately matched by the extended gesture of the vocal line; and each sonnet stands forth clearly, three-dimensionally, in its setting. Some of the sonnets—especially *Si comè nella penna e nell'inchiostro* (XVI) and *Spirto ben nato, in cui si specchia e vede* (XXIV)—are treated in a declamatory vein. In *Veggio co'bei vostri occhi un dolce lume* (XXX), the voice describes wide sweeping trajectories that are often at variance with the accompanying harmonies. In all these songs the piano seems deliberately to sacrifice most of its polyphonic potentialities and to concentrate as far as possible on a simple, single-minded partnership with the voice. The various sonnets are well contrasted with each other in tempo, mood and key; but, except in the case of sonnet XXXII, there is a not unnatural tendency for the phrasing to coincide with the quatrain or terzet or even with the individual line and to produce a certain uniformity or even monotony of pattern.

These *Sonnets* were written specially for Peter Pears and were an immediate success on their first performance by him with the composer at the piano (Wigmore Hall, September, 1942).

The *Hymn to St. Cecilia* was intended to help restore the old custom of celebrating on November 22 (Britten's birthday) the feast of the patron saint of music—a custom that had been regularly observed in former centuries. Auden's invocation to the saint fully deserves to take its place among the odes of Nicholas Brady and John Dryden as set by Purcell and Handel:

> *Blessed Cecilia, appear in visions*
> *To all musicians, appear and inspire;*
> *Translated Daughter, come down and startle*
> *Composing mortals with immortal fire.*

And listening mortals were certainly startled when on St. Cecilia's Day, 1942, the *Hymn* was performed for the first time by the B.B.C. Singers conducted by Leslie Woodgate. The work as a whole made an impression of simplicity, delicacy, sweetness and tranquillity—qualities that are rare in the music of this confused and unhappy age and were not altogether expected from a composer who before his visit to the United States had acquired a reputation for precocious sophistication. The sweet and languid harmonies of the opening invocation, the brisk scherzo ('*I cannot grow*') with its light broken movement, the candid beauty of the soprano solo, '*O dear white children casual as birds*', and the group of gay cadenzas where the voices flamboyantly imitate violin, drum, flute and trumpet in turn—all these episodes combined to form a work that gave great pleasure and satisfaction to listeners and performers alike.

A Ceremony of Carols was first performed by the Fleet Street Choir, conducted by T. B. Lawrence, in Norwich Castle on December 5, 1942. In some ways it is a pendant to *A Boy was Born*; but whereas the earlier work was in the form of a theme followed by six variations and finale for mixed voices unaccompanied, *A Ceremony of Carols* is written for treble voices (generally divided into three parts with occasional solo passages) accompanied by harp and consists of a sequence of eight separate carols framed by a Procession and Recession with an interlude for harp solo placed about two-thirds of the way through. As with the earlier work, the words are drawn mainly from anonymous medieval carols; but there are also settings of poems by James, John and Robert Wedderburn, Robert Southwell and William Cornish. The separate numbers are effectively matched and contrasted with each other; and though the work is in some ways less ambitious than *A Boy was Born*, it is perhaps more successful and even more spontaneous than the earlier composition.

Whereas formerly the Church was a powerful patron of the arts, in recent years the divorce between it and the artist has become unfortunately accentuated—to the detriment of both parties. It is always pleasant to find an exception—a church that recognizes the importance of the living artist and is prepared to employ him and display his work in the unique setting of its building; and during the last few years one of the most striking examples of such enlightened patronage in England has been provided by the Church of St. Matthew, Northampton. The commissions placed through its incumbent, the Rev. Walter Hussey, have included a statue of the Madonna and Child by Henry Moore, a mural painting of the Crucifixion by Graham Sutherland, and a Festival Cantata written by Britten to commemorate the fiftieth anniversary (on September 21, 1943) of the Church's consecration.

For this Cantata, Britten selected a number of passages from *Rejoice in the Lamb*, that strange eighteenth century poem written by Christopher Smart, while he was in a madhouse. This work is a canticle of general praise, in which not only 'nations and languages', but also 'every creature in which is the breath of life', including the poet's favourite cat, Jeoffrey, and the mouse 'a creature of great personal valour', unite in praising God and rejoicing in their service :

> *Hallelujah from the heart of God*
> *And from the hand of the artist inimitable*
> *And from the echo of the heavenly harp*
> *In sweetness magnifical and mighty.*

The music matches the thrilling visionary quality of the words, being simple, clear and bold. It reveals in Britten a compassion with the poet himself and also with the objects of the poet's compassion that is particularly moving.

A similar commission a short time afterwards led to the composition of a small-scale *Te Deum* to commemorate the Centenary Festival of the Church of St. Mark, Swindon (April 24, 1945).

Another occasional work was the *Prelude and Fugue* for 18-part string orchestra, written specially for the tenth anniversary of the Boyd Neel Orchestra and performed at the Wigmore Hall on June 23, 1943.

The following year his earlier work for strings, *Simple Symphony*, took on a new lease of life when it was used by Walter Gore (at the suggestion of David Martin) for a light essay in abstract dancing; and it was first performed in this guise by the Ballet Rambert at the Theatre Royal, Bristol (November 19, 1944).

But of more importance from the point of view of the opera he had agreed to write for Koussevitsky were the *Serenade* for tenor solo, horn and string orchestra (first performed by Peter Pears and Dennis Brain with Walter Goehr and his orchestra at the Wigmore Hall on October 15, 1943) and the incidental music to Edward Sackville-West's radio play, *The Rescue*.

The *Serenade* is written to almost the same scale as *Les Illuminations;* but this time Britten has chosen an English instead of a French text, and Rimbaud's fragmentary, half-apprehended visions give way to an exquisitely selected miniature anthology that includes the Lyke Wake Dirge, lyrics by Cotton, Tennyson, Blake and Ben Jonson, and as finale a sonnet by Keats. In the words of Edward Sackville-West,[1] to whom the *Serenade* is dedicated: 'The subject is Night and its prestigia: the lengthening shadow, the distant bugle at sunset, the Baroque panoply of the starry sky, the heavy angels of sleep; but also the cloak of evil—the worm in the heart of the rose, the sense of sin in the heart of man. The whole sequence forms an Elegy or Nocturnal (as Donne would have called it), resuming the thoughts and images suitable to evening.' Just as *A Ceremony of Carols* was framed by a Procession and Recession, the *Serenade* has a horn solo that is played on natural harmonics as Prologue and repeated off-stage as Epilogue.

Two movements call for special notice. In the Sonnet (Keats), the horn is silent, and soft string chords accompany a vocal *arioso* of great beauty. Where in the *Michelangelo Sonnets* Britten seemed not always to have discovered a completely satisfactory musical solvent for the sonnet form, here not only is the special relation of octave to sestet faithfully reflected in the music, but the musical enjambment of the five-beat lines, the metrical variety and subtlety displayed in setting the words, and the wide range and sensitivity of the vocal line are sufficient to show that music is fully capable of assimilating so intricate a verse form and producing an integument of like intensity, richness, discipline and overall unity.

Diametrically opposite to this process is Britten's treatment of the Elegy. *The Sick Rose*, taken from *Songs of Experience*, is one of Blake's shortest and most pregnant lyrics.

---

[1]'Music: Some Aspects of the Contemporary Problem' by Edward Sackville-West. *Horizon*, June, July and August, 1944.

O Rose, thou art sick !
The invisible worm
That flies in the night,
In the howling storm,

Has found out thy bed
Of crimson joy;
And his dark secret love
Does thy life destroy.

Though ostensibly in two stanzas, it cannot be set in stanzaic form without breaking the single sentence in half and mutilating its meaning. On the other hand, any type of musical setting that causes undue prolongation of syllables or repetition of words or phrases will immediately destroy the poem's wonderful simplicity and terseness. This lyric is only a quarter of the length of a sonnet: yet its dramatic implications are fully as great. Britten's solution was to take the drama of the invisible worm and its burrowings in the heart of the rose as cue for an instrumental movement where the horn accompanied by strings provides an ideal setting in musical, not poetic, time for the unheard words. This movement is broken for eight bars in the middle by a passage of recitative for the tenor accompanied only by the cellos; and in this way the lyric, when it comes, is delivered with maximum clarity and effect. Some people may complain that the composer has solved this problem only by evading it; but in view of the brilliant use to which the same device was to be put in the composition of *Peter Grimes*, it would be juster to agree with Edward Sackville-West when he says:[1] 'Only an imagination of a very rare kind could have hit on this solution to the problem. Within its limits, this is a revolutionary way of setting a lyric.'

Simultaneously with his work on the *Serenade*, Britten found time to collaborate with Edward Sackville-West,

---

[1] Edward Sackville-West *op. cit.*

who was writing a melodrama for broadcasting based on Homer's *Odyssey* and entitled *The Rescue*. In the Preamble to the published text, the author explains that he was experimenting with a form of radio-opera or radio-drama and 'in writing *The Rescue* some of the awkwardnesses incident to radio-drama were automatically removed . . . by the operatic nature of the composition, which was deliberately built upon an hypothetical structure of music'.[1] This meant that the composer was given many opportunities, which included passages of speech-music, instrumental solos associated with various characters, a vocal quartet of gods and goddesses, and brief transitional passages for orchestra between the scenes. Here again Britten's flair for descriptive music did not desert him. Describing the course of their collaboration, Sackville-West has paid him this tribute: 'I was continually struck by the unerring instinct with which Britten hit upon the right musical backing for whatever it was I had written, or—alternatively—rose imaginatively to any occasion the script presented for quasi-independent music.' *The Rescue* was first performed by the B.B.C. in two parts on November 25 and 26, 1943.

By now Britten had found a librettist for his opera. While still in the United States, he had thought of asking Christopher Isherwood; but after his return to England, it was clear that the choice would have to fall on someone who was living in England. He already knew Montagu Slater as a poet and dramatist—in fact, in 1938 he had written incidental music for two one-act verse plays of his, *The Seven Ages of Man* and *Old Spain*, which were performed that summer as puppet plays at the Mercury Theatre, London, by the Binyon Puppets—and now he asked him to prepare a libretto that would be based on Crabbe's poem, *The Borough*, and give special prominence

---

[1] *The Rescue*: a melodrama for broadcasting based on Homer's *Odyssey*, by Edward Sackville-West. Secker & Warburg, 1945.

to the character of Peter Grimes. The writing of the text, together with its revisions and corrections, took about eighteen months, and by the end of 1943 all was ready for Britten to begin the work of composition.

Before settling down to this long and arduous job, however, he remembered there were friends of his in a Prisoners-of-War Camp at Eichstätt in Germany who were planning a musical festival early in the new year, and he composed a special work for them, the score of which was sent out page by page in microfilm letter form. According to Richard Wood, who organized the festival: '*The Ballad of Little Musgrave and Lady Barnard* for male voices and pianos by Benjamin Britten and dedicated to the musicians of OFLAG VII B arrived just in time for us to put it into the programme at the end of the festival (which had started on February 18, 1944). Our resources and capabilities were brilliantly envisioned by the composer and the result was a little work (eight to nine minutes) of great dramatic force. The choir enjoyed singing it enormously in the end, though it was quite foreign to their style. We gave it four times.'

Britten began composing the music of *Peter Grimes* in January, 1944; and the score was completed by February of the following year. The question of its production in England was naturally one that exercised his mind. Although opera in Italian had formed a regular part of London's musical diet since the beginning of the 18th century, opera in English had never had a real opportunity of taking root in England, partly because until comparatively recent years little or nothing had been done to familiarize the people living outside London with opera, and partly also because for this and other reasons it had never proved possible to establish permanent companies of the requisite status and stability.

Before the war, it was customary for some special organization or syndicate to arrange an annual eight to ten weeks' season of opera in German, Italian and sometimes French at Covent Garden, while it was left to a long established company like the Carl Rosa (founded in 1875) to tour English versions of the more popular operas through the provinces. During this period a kind of English *Volks-oper* was growing up, first at the Old Vic Theatre in the Waterloo Road, London, and after 1931 at Sadler's Wells. This company presented not only operas in English—many of them in Edward J. Dent's excellent translations—but also English operas; and before the outbreak of the war it had to its credit productions of Stanford's *The Travelling Companion*, Dame Ethel Smyth's *The Wreckers*, Holst's *Savitri* and Vaughan Williams' *Hugh the Drover* among others. Although after the onset of the German air attacks on London in September, 1940, the Sadler's Wells Theatre was closed to the public and used as a rest-centre for evacuees, the opera company just managed to avoid complete disintegration. At first it toured the provinces with a scratch company of twenty-five (including the orchestra!) playing simplified versions of operas like *The Marriage of Figaro* and *La Traviata;* but soon, emboldened by the eager response it evoked, it began to build up its singers, chorus and orchestra and to enlarge its repertory. At the time Britten and Pears returned to England from America, the Sadler's Wells Opera Company under the direction of Joan Cross had made the New Theatre, London, its head-quarters; and in 1943 Peter Pears joined it and was soon singing leading parts in *Così fan tutte*, *La Traviata*, *The Bartered Bride* and other operas.

In February 1944, in the course of an interview, Britten said:[1] 'I am passionately interested in seeing a successful permanent national opera in existence—successful both artistically and materially. And it must be vital and contemporary, too, and depend less on imported "stars" than

---

[1] 'Conversation with Benjamin Britten.' *Tempo*, February 1944.

on a first-rate, young and fresh, permanent company. Sadler's Wells have made a good beginning.' A few months later, thanks largely to the enthusiastic support of the Opera Director, Joan Cross, it was agreed that *Peter Grimes* when completed should be given its first performance by the Sadler's Wells Company and that this production should mark the Company's return to its own theatre, which had now been derequisitioned. The certainty of production—and at an early date—was a fresh incentive to Britten (if one were needed) to finish the score; and, as he later admitted,[1] 'the qualities of the Opera Company considerably influenced both the shape and the characterization of the opera'.

Rehearsals began on tour—according to Eric Crozier[2] 'in a Methodist Hall in Sheffield, in a Birmingham gymnasium and in the Civic Hall at Wolverhampton. They were as thorough as circumstances could allow, with a company exhausted by much travel and busy with eight performances each week of other operas'. But, despite all difficulties, the production was ready on time; and so it came about that on June 7, 1945, a month after the capitulation of Germany, Sadler's Wells Theatre reopened with a world first performance of a new English opera. Peter Pears sang the title role; Joan Cross herself appeared as Ellen Orford; the parts of Auntie, Balstrode, Mrs. Sedley and Swallow were taken by Edith Coates, Roderick Jones, Valetta Iacopi and Owen Brannigan respectively. The scenery and costumes by Kenneth Green were in an attractively realistic style; Eric Crozier produced; and the orchestra was conducted by Reginald Goodall.

Whatever apprehensions may have been felt beforehand by the composer, by those concerned in the production, by

---

[1] *Peter Grimes: Sadler's Wells Opera Books No.* 3.

[2] *The Rape of Lucretia* (commemorative volume) ed. Eric Crozier. The Bodley Head, 1948.

executants or audience, were all swept away as the actual performance proceeded. The orchestra might be too small to do full justice to the interludes, the stage space too cramped for the action, the idiom of the music unfamiliar, the principals and chorus under-rehearsed, yet the impact of the work was so powerful that when the final chorus reached its climax and the curtain began to fall slowly, signifying not only the end of the opera but also the beginning of another day in the life of the Borough, all who were present realized that *Peter Grimes*, as well as being a masterpiece of its kind, marked the beginning of an operatic career of great promise and perhaps also the dawn of a period when English opera would flourish in its own right.

CHAPTER V

First Operatic Successes

The success of *Peter Grimes* was immediate and decisive. The London production was followed during the next three years by others in Stockholm, Basle, Antwerp, Zurich, Tanglewood, Milan, Hamburg, Mannheim, Berlin, Brno, Graz, Copenhagen, Budapest, New York, Stanford and Oldenburg[1] so that within a comparatively short time Britten's fame as an opera-composer was world-wide, and it became a matter of general interest to know what sort of an opera he was going to write next.

With the end of the war, however, the unstable operatic picture in Great Britain continued to shift and change. Perhaps the most important new factor was the avowed intention of a number of public-spirited persons to reopen the Royal Opera House, Covent Garden, which had been used as a dance-hall during the war years, and to run it as a national lyric theatre for opera and ballet. Messrs. Boosey & Hawkes, the music publishers, took a lease of the building from the ground landlords and sub-let the theatre to a special Trust that was set up with Lord Keynes as its first Chairman. Financial backing from the State, which had never before shown any real interest in opera, was secured through the Arts Council; and immediate steps were taken to obtain resident opera and ballet companies. The Sadler's Wells Ballet, which had been created by Ninette de Valois and built up carefully during the last fifteen years from quite humble beginnings, accepted an invitation from the Covent Garden Trust to become its resident ballet company and gave a magnificent performance of Tchaikovsky's *Sleeping Beauty* at the gala reopening on February 20, 1946; but as no existing English opera company seemed

[1]See Appendix B.

suitable for transfer to Covent Garden, the Trustees decided to form their own company from scratch. Clearly it would take some time to assemble and train the singers; and, in actual fact, the first performance of the new company was not given until January 1947.

Meanwhile, the general outlook was uncertain. *Peter Grimes* was withdrawn from the Sadler's Wells repertory in March 1946, after twenty-four performances; and it seemed unlikely that the company would be able to produce any new English operas in the near future. In Britten's own words:[1] 'To some of the singers, writers and musicians involved in *Peter Grimes* this appeared to be the moment to start a group dedicated to the creation of new works, performed with the least possible expense and capable of attracting new audiences by being toured all over the country.' Accordingly, a new company was planned with the object of providing opportunities for the composition and performance of works that would forego the apparatus of large orchestras and choruses. As was explained in a preliminary manifesto:[2] 'The practical aim behind the formation of the Glyndebourne English Opera Company is towards providing a method by which singers of the first rank can devote five months of each year between June and October—slack months in the concert world—entirely to the rehearsal and performance of opera. . . . The principal belief that has inspired the creation of the new English Opera Company is that it is possible and desirable to develop a kind of British opera that will explore the vital native qualities of the English voice and language. For this, the clear singing of good English will be an essential.' The scale of the new venture was to be kept as small as possible

---

[1]Special programme note by Benjamin Britten for the Salzburg Festival performance of *The Rape of Lucretia*, 1950.

[2]'Benjamin Britten's Second Opera' by Eric Crozier. *Tempo*, March 1946.

—at least to begin with—since it was only thus that 'the principles of high quality in singing, musicianship and preparation can be reconciled with the regular performance of new works'. To speed this venture, Britten agreed to write a new opera for eight singers and twelve musicians, to be produced by the Company at Glyndebourne for a limited run in the summer of 1946 and then to be taken on tour to the provinces and to London.

It happened that a friend of his, Ronald Duncan, had just written a verse play, *This Way to the Tomb*, in the form of a masque with anti-masque—the first part showing how in the fourteenth century Father Antony, Abbot of St. Ferrara on the island of Zante, withdrew to a mountain height with the firm resolve of fasting unto death, but was there assailed by various temptations, including the deadly sin of pride, and the second part depicting a television relay from the saint's tomb some five centuries later and the unacceptable miracle of the saint's return to life. For its production at the Mercury Theatre on October 11, 1945, Britten wrote incidental music—liturgical chants for a four-part choir using the Latin words of Psalm 69 and a Franciscan hymn, two songs with piano accompaniment for one of the novitiates, and various bits of jazz for piano (four-handed) and percussion in the television scene. These numbers were so well contrived that it was legitimate to claim that the play owed a considerable part of its success to Britten's music; and it was not unexpected, therefore, when this collaboration was carried a stage further by Duncan being invited to write the libretto for Britten's next opera, *The Rape of Lucretia*, the subject of which had already been suggested by Eric Crozier.

Meanwhile, Britten had celebrated the completion of the score of *Peter Grimes* by plunging into the composition of various new works. At the beginning of August 1945, just after his return from a tour of Belsen and other German concentration camps which he had undertaken as Yehudi Menuhin's accompanist, he set nine of the *Holy Sonnets of John Donne* for high voice and piano and followed this up by finishing his second String Quartet on October 14, both works being written as an act of homage to commemorate the 250th anniversary of the death of Henry Purcell which fell on November 21 of that year.

The Holy Sonnets of John Donne stand nearer to the *Seven Sonnets of Michelangelo* than to the Keats Sonnet in the *Serenade;* and over and above their Baroque display of rhetoric, they reveal a facility for musical conceits that not only closely matches the sombre metaphysical imagery of Donne's poetry with its agony of repentance in the shadow of death, but also recalls the fanciful and unorthodox side of Purcell's peculiar genius as well. Clearly, Britten's work as concert pianist and accompanist since his return from America had helped to familiarize him with the music of Purcell; and it might be said of him that, like Purcell, he never failed to 'find for words a music that exists in its own right as music'. This tribute is particularly true of the last Sonnet in the sequence, '*Death be not proud*', which, constructed as a *passacaglia* with a firm muscular ground bass, successfully embraces extremes, being both simple and fanciful, sensuous and austere, a masterpiece of feeling and form.

The second String Quartet is Britten's most ambitious attempt since the Piano and Violin Concertos to write a work in which form would be dictated, not by extraneous ideas, but by inner musical necessity. The result is a most impressive essay in sonata form expressed in terms of contemporary idiom. The first movement (*Allegro calmo senza rigore*) consists of the exposition, development and recapitulation of three themes, each of which starts with an upward leap of the interval of a major tenth—almost as if the maladjustment of Peter Grimes, which is so often characterized in the opera by the interval of a ninth, had at last found its musical resolution. A sombre scherzo (*Vivace*) with muted strings separates this from the final movement, with its Purcellian title of Chacony, which (to quote from Erwin Stein's excellent analysis[1]) 'consists of a theme and twenty-one variations. They are arranged in four groups, each of which is separated from the next by a cadenza. The first group contains the theme (unison) and six different harmonizations. The second group brings six rhythmical variations. In the third group, again in six sections, the theme is played as accompaniment to a melody which itself is being varied. The last group of three variations forms the coda'.

Britten's interest in Purcell was by no means transitory. Shortly after the commemoration concert of November 21, 1945, he planned jointly with Peter Pears a performing edition of some of Purcell's works, for which he realized the figured bass with characteristic ingenuity and invention. The first volumes of this edition started to appear in 1946 and included the Golden Sonata and selections from *Orpheus Britannicus*, *Odes and Elegies* and Playford's *Harmonia Sacra*. He also chose a theme of Purcell's for the air on which he intended to construct a set of variations to accompany a Ministry of Education film on the instruments of the orchestra; and a new performing edition of *Dido and Aeneas* was planned and advertised in the 1946 Glyndebourne programme for production there the following year, though in fact the project did not materialize until 1951.

Before settling down to the task of composing *The Rape of Lucretia*, he allowed himself the relaxation of writing incidental music to *The Dark Tower*, a radio parable play by Louis MacNeice inspired by Robert Browning's poem,

---

[1] *Analysis of String Quartet No. 2 in C* by Erwin Stein. Boosey & Hawkes, 1946.

'*Childe Roland to the Dark Tower Came*'. This was first broadcast in the B.B.C. Home Service on January 21, 1946, with Britten's music played by a string orchestra of twenty-six players, together with percussion and one trumpet. The author's attitude to the composer's score was enthusiastic. 'Benjamin Britten', he wrote, 'provided this programme with music which is, I think, the best I have heard in a radio play. Without his music *The Dark Tower* lacks a dimension.'

The greater part of the winter and spring of 1946—apart from a concert tour with Peter Pears to Holland and Belgium—was taken up with the composition of *The Rape;* and during this period Britten collaborated closely, not only with his librettist, but also with Eric Crozier and John Piper, who had been chosen as producer and designer respectively. Rehearsals started at Glyndebourne in June; and the first performance was given on July 12 with Ernest Ansermet as conductor. A first-rate double cast had been assembled, the parts of Lucretia, Tarquinius, and the Male and Female Chorus being taken on alternate nights by Kathleen Ferrier and Nancy Evans, Otakar Kraus and Frank Rogier, Peter Pears and Aksel Schiotz, Joan Cross and Flora Nielsen. Reginald Goodall alternated as conductor with Ansermet.

In this production, special praise should be given to the work of John Piper as designer. The double arcade setting used for the second scenes of Acts I and II was particularly memorable, though, as he himself has admitted,[1] its parallel arrangement was 'in essence pictorial or architectural rather than theatrical, and it threw a heavy burden on the producer if he was to make the scenes played in front of these arcades "work" in an interesting and lively way'. A real triumph was his drop cloth for Act II, the deep glowing and smouldering colours of which, depicting Our Lord in

---

[1] *The Rape of Lucretia* (commemorative volume) ed. Eric Crozier.

Majesty, recalled the best English stained glass of the thir-
teenth and fourteenth centuries.

Some of the critics who reviewed *The Rape* seemed to
have difficulty in accepting the premises of the work. Looking for the mass effects of a second *Peter Grimes*, they
found instead an opera built on austere chamber music
lines, without a large chorus or orchestra. The Christian
commentary of the single figures who act as Male and
Female Chorus was objected to as a wilful anachronism,
while the didactic tone of some of their historical information about the Romans and Etruscans—references that for
the most part were modified or expunged in the revised
version of 1947—was resented as an intrusion. Yet there
was no doubt that the audience's attention was held
throughout, carried along on the gentle swell of the first
act, gripped by the hastening motion of the arching, then
breaking wave of the action as it passed from Lucretia's
rape to her suicide in Act II, and soothed by the slow with-
drawal of the final sextet and the Chorus's exergue; and by
the end of the summer the opera had been played about
seventy-five times in Great Britain, the 100th performance
being celebrated at Covent Garden on October 17 the
following year.

When the tour to Manchester, Liverpool, Edinburgh,
Glasgow, London (Sadler's Wells), Oxford and Holland
was over, Britten and his supporters decided to relaunch
the company the following year under the title of the
English Opera Group. Although now independent of
Glyndebourne, the Group would perform there as visitors
in June 1947. Its aims and objects were restated by its
promotors in the following terms: 'We believe the time has
come when England, which has never had a tradition of
native opera, but has always depended on a repertory of
foreign works, can create its own operas. . . . This Group
will give annual seasons of contemporary opera in English

and suitable classical works including those of Purcell. It is part of the Group's purpose to encourage young composers to write for the operatic stage, also to encourage poets and playwrights to tackle the problem of writing libretti in collaboration with composers.' It was made clear that concerts as well as opera preformances would come within its purview; and the new works commissioned for 1947 were, accordingly, an opera by Britten and a *Stabat Mater* by Lennox Berkeley.

Immediately after *The Rape of Lucretia*'s short initial run at Glyndebourne, Britten was invited to attend the first American production of *Peter Grimes* at Koussevitsky's Berkshire Music Centre at Tanglewood, Lennox, Massachusetts (August 6, 7 and 8). On his return, he wrote an Occasional Overture in C for the opening orchestral concert of the new B.B.C. Third Programme at the end of September. Later he decided to withdraw this composition, and it does not figure in his list of published works. About the same time he provided incidental music for Carl Czinner's New York production of Webster's *The Duchess of Malfi*, with Elizabeth Bergner in the title role, and on New Year's Eve completed *The Young Person's Guide to the Orchestra*.

The latter work was designed to form the sound track for an educational film entitled *Instruments of the Orchestra*, showing the orchestra as a whole, its four departments and the individual instruments; but it is written in such a way that it can be played as a concert piece as well, with or without spoken commentary. It is planned in the form of variations and a fugue on a dance tune from Purcell's incidental music to *Abdelazar, or The Moor's Revenge*. There are six statements of the theme—for full orchestra, for woodwind, brass, strings and percussion separately, and then for full orchestra again—and thirteen variations for (i) flutes and piccolo, (ii) oboes, (iii) clarinets, (iv) bassoons, (v) violins,

(vi) violas, (vii) cellos, (viii) double basses, (ix) harp, (x) horns, (xi) trumpets, (xii) trombones and bass tuba, and (xiii) the various percussion instruments. In the fugue, the instruments make their entries in the same order; and finally the brass recapitulates the theme, while the rest of the orchestra continues playing the fugue. Every point in this lucid musical exposition is made with such directness and precision that the work has become a kind of standard *vademecum* for the young listener.

In the winter of 1947, Britten undertook another Continental tour. He visited Zurich and there conducted performances of the *Serenade* and *The Young Person's Guide to the Orchestra* and, together with Peter Pears, gave song recitals in Switzerland, Holland, Belgium and Scandinavia. On returning to England, he settled down to the composition of his new opera for the English Opera Group. Here the problem confronting him and his librettist, Eric Crozier, was how to devise an opera made to the same measure as *The Rape of Lucretia*, but as different as possible in subject matter and style—in fact, a comedy instead of a tragedy, with a late nineteenth century instead of a B.C. setting. Guy de Maupassant's short story, *Le Rosier de Madame Husson*, gave them the basic idea; but the Gallic original was so freely adapted into East Anglian terms that the resulting lyrical comedy, *Albert Herring*, which was performed for the first time at Glyndebourne on June 20, had much of the flavour of an original work.

Once again, scenery and costumes were entrusted to John Piper—with excellent results. Particularly admired were the scene in Mrs. Herring's greengrocery in Loxford and the drop curtain showing the market-place with the rich fuscous gloom of its buildings enlivened only by the newly painted signboard of its inn glowing like a drop of blood. Frederick Ashton, widely known for his work as choreographer to the Sadler's Wells Ballet, produced. A first-rate cast was assembled, including Peter Pears in the title role and Joan Cross as Lady Billows, an elderly regal autocrat; and Britten himself conducted.

Before the Glyndebourne season closed, *The Rape of Lucretia* was revived in a revised version; and both operas were included in the English Opera Group's tour abroad to the International Festival at Scheveningen, the Stadsschouwburg in Amsterdam and the Lucerne International Festival. During their visit to Switzerland, a concert was given at Zurich, at which Lennox Berkeley's *Stabat Mater* was performed for the first time; and back in England, they gave ten opera performances at Covent Garden and toured to Newcastle upon Tyne, Bournemouth and Oxford before dispersing for the winter.

Meanwhile, the Covent Garden Opera Company had prepared a new production of *Peter Grimes* under the direction of Tyrone Guthrie. This opened on November 6, with Peter Pears and Joan Cross as guest artists singing their original parts; and, after a few performances, their roles were taken over by Richard Lewis and Doris Doree. New scenery and costumes had been designed by Tanya Moiseiwitch; but whereas Eric Crozier's production and Kenneth Green's designs at Sadler's Wells had been in a realistic vein (as specified in Montagu Slater's libretto), Tyrone Guthrie and Tanya Moiseiwitch had decided on a more abstract interpretation of the drama. The main Borough set, as used in the first scenes of Acts I and II and the whole of Act III, showed a spacious beach and implied an illimitable sea beyond, but left the Moot Hall, the church and *The Boar* entirely to the imagination. This meant that the dance at the beginning of Act III, which, with its four-piece band, is supposed to take place off-stage in the Moot Hall, was given on the beach in full view of the audience, a change which was not altogether an improvement. It must also be admitted that on the vast stage of Covent Garden the scene in *The Boar* failed to produce that feeling of claustrophily which is so characteristic of English pubs. But, apart from these small reservations, the production was a fine one, and it was specially admired in Brussels and Paris when the Covent Garden Company played there the following June.

When *Peter Grimes* was revived at Covent Garden five years later (November 14, 1953) in a new production by John Cranko, the sets were adapted by Roger Ramsdell and many of the weaknesses of the earlier version were eradicated.

CHAPTER VI

Festival Interlude

In 1947 Britten moved from Snape to Aldeburgh. There he took a house overlooking the sea that Crabbe had described so lovingly in *The Borough*:

> *Various and vast, sublime in all its forms,*
> *When lull'd by Zephyrs, or when rous'd by Storms,*
> *Its colours changing, when from Clouds and Sun*
> *Shades after shades upon the surface run.*

Shortly after the move he was driving by car from Holland to Switzerland with his friends Peter Pears and Eric Crozier. The English Opera Group had just played *The Rape of Lucretia* and *Albert Herring* at the Holland Festival and was due to appear a few days later at the Lucerne Festival. Eric Crozier has described[1] how the three of them felt 'proud that England was at last making some contribution to the traditions of international opera. And yet—there was something absurd about travelling so far to win success with British operas that Manchester, Edinburgh and London would not support. The cost of transporting forty people and their scenery was enormously high: despite packed houses in Holland, despite financial support from the British Council in Switzerland, it looked as if we should lose at least £3,000 on twelve Continental performances. It was exciting to represent British music at international festivals, but we could not hope to repeat the experiment another year.' It was at this point that Peter Pears had an inspiration. 'Why not make our own Festival?' he suggested. 'A modest Festival with a few concerts given by friends? Why not have an Aldeburgh Festival?'

---

[1]'The Origin of the Aldeburgh Festival' by Eric Crozier. *The Aldeburgh Festival Programme Book*, 1948.

During the following autumn and winter the idea was submitted to the local population, who greeted it with enthusiasm; and although Aldeburgh has only about two and a half thousand inhabitants, £1,400 was subscribed in advance guarantees. The programme was carefully planned; the artistic direction entrusted to the English Opera Group; and the first Aldeburgh Festival with the Earl of Harewood as President opened on June 5, 1948, and lasted for nine days.

The Festival was an immediate success and at once established itself on an annual basis. It has the merit of being local in the best sense. Aldeburgh itself is an unique setting for the arts. Britten's compositions naturally play an important part in the programmes; and both he and Peter Pears appear as executants. There is an Aldeburgh Festival Choir whose members are drawn from the neighbourhood; and lectures and exhibitions, usually on East Anglian themes, supplement the opera performances, concerts and recitals. Attendances at the Festival are limited by the accommodation Aldeburgh can offer—particularly the capacity of the Jubilee Hall, where the opera performances and some of the concerts are given. This holds no more than 300; so, in default of any larger building to accommodate its main events, the Festival is bound to remain small and intimate in scale.

It might be thought that this would tend to make it exclusive and even a little snobbish; but the fact that it is welcomed equally by the local inhabitants and visitors shows that this danger has been avoided. In his broadcast talk, *Looking Back on the First Aldeburgh Festival*,[1] E. M. Forster had a revealing anecdote to tell about the first performance of *Albert Herring* in the Jubilee Hall. 'During the first interval a man in a pub said: "I took a ticket for

---

[1] Reprinted in *The Aldeburgh Festival Programme Book*, 1949.

this show because it is local and I felt I had to. I'd have sold it to anyone for sixpence earlier on. I wouldn't part with it now for ten pounds".'

There has been a distinguished succession of lecturers including E. M. Forster, William Plomer, Sir Kenneth Clark, Dr. Edith Sitwell, John Betjeman and W. H. Auden. Among modern artists whose work has been exhibited are Henry Moore, John Piper and John Nash. The Choir and Orchestra of the Rotterdam Volksuniversiteit and the Choir of Spangen were visitors to the 1950 Festival and performed Bach's *St. Matthew Passion*; and the Copenhagen Boys' Choir of the Royal Chapel gave a special choral concert in 1952. In addition to his regular appearances as a recitalist with Peter Pears, Britten also usually directs from the pianoforte a special eighteenth-century orchestral programme including one of the Mozart piano concertos.

A number of his works have received first performances at the Festival. The first festival of all (1948) opened with his cantata *Saint Nicolas* to words by Eric Crozier. This had been written during the winter of 1947–8 specially for the Centenary Celebrations of Lancing College in July 1948. Its lay-out for tenor, mixed choirs, string orchestra, pianoforte and percussion and the fact that it included two familiar hymns for congregation and choirs made it particularly suitable for performance at the Aldeburgh Parish Church. Movements like The Birth of Nicolas with the innocent and joyful lilt of the sopranos' tune answered at the end of each verse by the boy Nicolas's treble '*God be glorified!*' and the strangely primitive story of Nicolas and the Pickled Boys fully justified E. M. Forster's comment:[1] 'It was one of those triumphs outside the rules of art which only the great artist can achieve.'

---

[1]From *Looking Back on the First Aldeburgh Festival, op. cit.*

E

Lachrymae, Reflections on a Song of Dowland, a set of ten variations for viola and piano, was first performed by William Primrose and the composer at the 1950 Festival. The following year the *Six Metamorphoses after Ovid* for oboe solo were written for Joy Boughton and played by her at the open-air concert given on the Meare at Thorpeness. These short pieces take their place with Debussy's *Syrinx* and Strawinsky's Three Pieces for Clarinet Solo as being among the most outstanding compositions for an unaccompanied wind instrument that have been written in this century.

For the 1953 Festival a special work for string orchestra was commissioned. Six variations on the tune of *Sellenger's Round, or, The Beginning of the World* were written by Lennox Berkeley, Arthur Oldham, Humphrey Searle, Michael Tippett and William Walton as well as Britten himself. The identity of the actual composer of each movement was concealed at the festival performances and only revealed later.

At every festival there has been opera of some kind or other. *Let's Make an Opera!* received its first production at the 1949 Festival. There have been revivals in 1948, 1949, 1951 and 1953 of *Albert Herring*, an opera with so many local connotations that it always seems to be most at home in the Aldeburgh Jubilee Hall; *The Rape of Lucretia* in 1949; *The Beggar's Opera* (with some of the movements transposed so that the part of Macheath could be sung by a baritone instead of a tenor) in 1950; and *Dido and Aeneas* (in Britten's new realization) in 1951. In addition, Monteverdi's *Il Combattimento di Tancredi e Clorinda* was given in 1951 and Arthur Oldham's version of *Love in a Village* in 1952.

One of the great attractions of the Aldeburgh Festival is its intimacy. The things that stick in one's memory are the brief cool intervals between the acts of the operas spent on the edge of the beach, the private houses that hospitably throw their rooms, studios and gardens open to accommodate the exhibitions, and the sight of Britten himself ready for every emergency and prepared to compose, conduct, play the piano, turn over for a fellow performer, or introduce a lecturer, as the case may be, an exuberant and indefatigable festival host.

CHAPTER VII

Opera Composition Continued

Britten's life was now following a fairly regular annual pattern. There was always a new opera on the stocks; a limited number of other compositions could usually be squeezed in; there would be a certain number of engagements as conductor and pianist; a recital tour (usually with Peter Pears) at home or abroad; and each summer would bring the busy but refreshing interlude of the Aldeburgh Festival.

About the time of his move to Aldeburgh, he completed two vocal works: *Canticle I* and *A Charm of Lullabies*. The *Canticle*, a setting of a poem by Francis Quarles for tenor and piano, is a more extended composition for voice than any of the previous song-cycles. Peter Pears, writing just before *Canticle II* was composed, considered it to be 'Britten's finest piece of vocal music to date'.[1] He particularly praised the vocal line as being 'free, melismatic yet controlled, and independent throughout, whether as one of two or three parts in counterpoint or a melody with chordal accompaniment'. *A Charm of Lullabies* reverts to the earlier song-cycle pattern. Britten has chosen five contrasting lullabies—*A Cradle Song* (William Blake), *The Highland Balou* (Robert Burns), *Sephestia's Lullaby* (Robert Greene), *A Charm* (Thomas Randolph) and *The Nurse's Song* (John Philip)—and set them for mezzo-soprano and piano.

For the 1948 season of the English Opera Group, he decided to add to the company's repertory a new version, not of *Dido and Aeneas* as had been promised earlier, but of *The Beggar's Opera*. For this purpose, John Gay's text was

---

[1]'The Vocal Music' by Peter Pears in *Benjamin Britten: a commentary* (edited by Mitchell & Keller).

slightly revised by Tyrone Guthrie, while Britten, ignoring all the numerous versions of the score that had appeared during the last two and a quarter centuries, went back to the sixty-nine airs originally chosen by Dr. Pepusch and included all of them in his version except three. Since his return from America he had produced three volumes of folk song arrangements (two for the British Isles and one for France), which showed such sensitivity to the mood and mode of folk tunes and skill in their setting that it was hardly surprising he should now find himself attracted by the traditional tunes of *The Beggar's Opera*.

For the first performance at the Arts Theatre, Cambridge (May 24, 1948), Tyrone Guthrie was producer. Profiting by a hint in the original Prologue that the opera had previously been performed by the Company of Beggars in their 'great Room at St. Giles's', he set the whole opera in this 'great room', which for some reason or other he imagined as a laundry. Unfortunately, the atmosphere of this laundry with its piles of clothes, whether dirty or clean, proved stifling, rather than inspiring, and the production never succeeded in fulfilling the producer's entirely laudable aim of restoring the mordency of the original satire. Britten wrote the part of Macheath for tenor voice; and the role was admirably sung by Peter Pears. When the opera was revived two years later, the part was transposed for baritone; but the result was not altogether satisfactory, some of the buoyancy and sparkle of the score being thereby lost.

After a week's run in Cambridge where it was conducted by Britten himself and Ivan Clayton, the opera was played by the English Opera Group at the Holland Festival, the Cheltenham Festival of Contemporary Music, the Festival du Littoral Belgique, Birmingham and the Sadler's Wells Theatre and the People's Palace, London; and during the next two or three years it was produced in Austria, Switzerland and Germany as well.

Having produced a Young Person's Guide to the Orchestra, Britten seemed bound sooner or later to write a Young Person's Guide to Opera. The episodes in *Albert Herring* where the three children bounce their ball against the door of Mrs. Herring's greengrocery shop and where Miss Wordsworth rehearses them in their festive song were among the most successful passages in that comic opera and seemed to show that such a work might well be written so as to provide parts to be played by children themselves. He believed there were many children in the country who were natural musicians and actors and was anxious to help provide an outlet for their artistic talent. In this he was ably aided and abetted by Eric Crozier. *Let's Make an Opera!* was planned in two parts: the first part to show a group of children helping two or three of their elders to plan, write, compose and rehearse an opera; and the second part being the opera itself, *The Little Sweep*. The music of this one-act opera is not continuous, but consists of eighteen musical numbers, and there is a certain amount of spoken dialogue. It was an ingenious stroke on the part of the authors of this entertainment for young people to implicate the audience in the performance of *The Little Sweep* as well as the children on the stage and the three or four professional adults that are called for in the cast. *Let's Make an Opera!* was an immediate success on its first production at the second Aldeburgh Festival (June 14, 1949). The conductor, who plays such an important part in knitting together the different musical strands of this entertainment, was Norman del Mar; Basil Coleman produced; and the attractive setting was by John Lewis.

As will be seen from Appendix B, *The Little Sweep* is easily Britten's most popular opera to date. As well as many professional productions in Europe, America, Asia and Australia, there have been innumerable amateur performances all over the world, particularly in schools. It is too early as yet to assess the effect of all this; but Eric Crozier's words should be borne in mind: 'Many children write plays for their own performance. Few, I suspect, attempt opera. Perhaps, with the stimulus of an imaginative example before them, they may be prompted to explore the fascinating possibilities of expression and entertainment that it offers.'[1]

Britten continued to attract much attention abroad. By 1948 monographs on his work as a composer had appeared in France, Italy and Switzerland as well as Great Britain. In its first three years The English Opera Group had toured its productions of *The Rape of Lucretia*, *Albert Herring* and *The Beggar's Opera* to Holland, Belgium, Switzerland, Denmark and Norway. *Peter Grimes* reached the Scala, Milan, and the Opera, Paris, in 1947 and the Metropolitan Opera House, New York the following year. *The Rape of Lucretia* aroused considerable controversy when it was produced in America. In Chicago it was greeted by one of the local newspapers with the banner headline 'Bold, Bawdy and Beautiful'; but its run in New York at the end of 1947 came to an abrupt end after only twenty-three performances. On that occasion Olin Downes, music critic of the *New York Times*, performed a complete *volte face*. After attending the first night, he praised the work warmly; but a return visit led him to change his mind and he decided it was 'as arrant a piece of musico-dramatic twaddle as has been visited upon the public for years'.[2] Hostile criticism of Britten was also forthcoming from the U.S.S.R. The first All-Union Congress of Soviet Composers that met at Moscow from April 19–25, 1948, energetically denounced him as a formalist in music, together with Menotti, Mes-

---

[1]'An Opera for Young People' by Eric Crozier. *Times Educational Supplement*, March 19, 1949.

[2]See 'The Rape of Lucretia', *New York Times*, December 30, 1948, and 'Second Thoughts', *New York Times*, January 9, 1949.

siaen and Strawinsky. Nevertheless, *Peter Grimes* has been played several times behind the iron curtain, particularly at Budapest and Schwerin, and Communist newspapers have not been slow to point a Marxist moral from the work and the society it depicts.

During the autumn and winter of 1948–9 Britten was pre-occupied with the *Spring Symphony*, the first performance of which was given at the Holland Festival, Amsterdam (July 9, 1949) by kind permission of Koussevitzky, who conducted the first American performance at the Berkshire Festival in Tanglewood (August 13, 1949). For two years he had been planning such a work, 'a symphony not only dealing with the Spring itself, but with the progress of Winter to Spring and the reawakening of the earth and life which that means'.[1] Apparently his original intention had been to use medieval Latin verse for this purpose; but 'a re-reading of much English lyric verse and a particularly lovely Spring day in East Suffolk, the Suffolk of Constable and Gainsborough', led him to change his mind and to substitute for his choice of Latin verse an anthology of English poems.

The *Spring Symphony* is written for three soloists (soprano, alto and tenor), mixed chorus, boys' choir, and large orchestra, including a cow-horn and a vibraphone. 'It is in the traditional four movement shape of a symphony, but with the movements divided into shorter sections bound together by a similar mood or point of view. Thus after an introduction, which is a prayer, in Winter, for Spring to come, the first movements deal with the arrival of Spring, the cuckoo, the birds, the flowers, the sun and "May month's beauty"; the second movements paint the darker side of Spring—the fading violets, rain and night; the third is a series of dances, the love of young people; the

---

[1] 'A Note on the Spring Symphony' by Benjamin Britten. *Music Survey*, Spring, 1950.

fourth is a May-day Festival, a kind of bank holiday, which ends with the great thirteenth-century traditional song "*Sumer is i-cumen in*", sung or rather shouted by the boys.'[1]

Apart from the account of Elizabethan London in May extracted from Beaumont and Fletcher's *The Knight of the Burning Pestle* which forms the finale, the sentiments of this springtime anthology culled from Edmund Spenser, Thomas Nashe, George Peele, John Clare, John Milton, Robert Herrick, Henry Vaughan, Richard Barnefield, and Anon. would be without specific indication of time or period, were it not for the four stanzas extracted from Auden's poem '*Out on the lawn I lie in bed*'[2] where the lulled listener is suddenly startled by the prophetic reference to Poland and war. Britten shows great skill in setting all this heterogeneous material in a unified musical idiom and in ordering it so as to give the work the specific gravity of a symphony instead of the running lightness of a suite.

After the *Spring Symphony* the collaboration with Ronald Duncan was resumed. Britten had already written incidental music, not only for Duncan's verse play *This Way to the Tomb*, but also for his translation and adaptation of Jean Cocteau's play *The Eagle Has Two Heads*, which was produced by The Company of Four at the Lyric Theatre, Hammersmith, on September 4, 1946. Now he provided music for Duncan's new verse play, *Stratton*, which started a brief provincial tour at the Theatre Royal, Brighton, on October 3, 1949; and in addition, he asked Duncan to provide the words for *A Wedding Anthem* that he wished to compose for the wedding of the Earl of Harewood, who was now President of the English Opera Group as well as of the Aldeburgh Festival, and Miss Marion Stein. This work for soprano and tenor soli, choir and organ was performed at St. Mark's Church, North Audley Street, Lon-

[1] *Ibid.*
[2] From *Look Stranger!* 1936.

don, on September 29, 1949, by Joan Cross, Peter Pears and the Choir of St. Mark's which had recently sung a number of Britten's choral works, including the early *Te Deum* (in C major) and *A Boy was Born*.

Shortly after the Harewood wedding, which was attended by the King and Queen and many members of the Royal Family, Britten and Peter Pears left for a concert tour of America. They crossed to the West Coast of the United States; and, while in Hollywood, Britten saw Carl Ebert rehearsing *Albert Herring* for production by the University of Southern California. Back in England by Christmas, he started to think about his next opera. He had already chosen Herman Melville's posthumous story, *Billy Budd, Foretopman*, as the subject, and E. M. Forster and Eric Crozier had agreed to write the libretto jointly. The work of composition was begun in February 1950 and finished in the autumn of 1951.

Britten accepted a commission from the Arts Council of Great Britain for the opera to be produced in connection with the Festival of Britain, 1951; but for some time the destination of the new opera was uncertain. At first it was intended that it should be produced by the Sadler's Wells Opera Company at the 1951 Edinburgh Festival, and this was announced in September 1950. Two months later, however, Sadler's Wells decided they would have altogether to abandon the idea of producing it as it was likely to prove beyond their resources; and in December it was announced that *Billy Budd* would be definitely produced at the Royal Opera House, Covent Garden, in the autumn of 1951.

During the twenty months or so that *Billy Budd* was being composed, Britten allowed few extraneous matters to distract him. The only other compositions belonging to this period were the *Lachrymae* for viola and piano (1950) and the *Six Metamorphoses after Ovid* for oboe solo (1951), both performed for the first time at the Aldeburgh Festival, and a set of *Five Flower Songs* for mixed chorus unaccompanied, dedicated to Leonard and Dorothy Elmhirst of Dartington Hall on the occasion of their 25th wedding anniversary (April 3, 1950). He also found time to prepare a new realization of *Dido and Aeneas* for the English Opera Group's Festival of Britain season.

It so happened that about this period a number of ballets were adapted to existing scores of his. *Soirées Musicales* and *Matinées Musicales* were used once more for a ballet which was produced at the Théâtre de la Monnaie, Brussels, in 1948 under the title *Fantaisie Italienne*. The following June *The Young Person's Guide to the Orchestra* was used for a modern classical ballet *Oui ou Non? (Ballet de la Paix)* presented by the Association des Amis de la Danse at their annual gala performance at the Théâtre National Populaire du Palais de Chaillot, Paris. On April 26, 1949, the Ballets de Paris de Roland Petit gave the first performance at the Prince's Theatre, London, of *Le Rêve de Léonor*, a surrealist ballet with choreography by Frederick Ashton to the *Variations on a Theme of Frank Bridge* arranged for full orchestra by Arthur Oldham. The same *Variations* were used in Lew Christensen's *Jinx*, the revised version of which was included in the New York City Ballet's repertory for its spring 1950 season and brought to this country when the New York City Ballet visited Covent Garden in July 1950. The same company performed *Les Illuminations* as a ballet at City Center, New York, on March 2, 1950, with choreography by Frederick Ashton and décor by Cecil Beaton; and this too was performed at Covent Garden in the summer. The *Sinfonietta* was used for a little drama in ballet form called *Die Versunkene Stadt* with choreography by Mara Jovanovits that was given at the Stadtheater, St. Gallen, Switzerland, on April 26, 1950.

The production of Purcell's *Dido and Aeneas* by the English Opera Group represented the fulfilment of a long cherished ambition. Before working out his own realization of the thorough bass, however, Britten collated and compared all the extant manuscript material and copied the whole of the transcript made by John Travers about twenty-five years after Purcell's death and preserved in the Library of St. Michael's College, Tenbury.[1] He then examined Nahum Tate's printed libretto and was particularly struck by the fact that no setting by Purcell exists for the witches' chorus and dance at the end of Act II. In a note dated April 4, 1951, which was printed in the Hammersmith programme, he wrote:

'Anyone who has taken part in, or indeed heard a concert or stage performance, must have been struck by the very peculiar and most unsatisfactory end of this Act II as it stands; Aeneas sings his very beautiful recitative in A minor and disappears without any curtain music or chorus (which occurs in all the other acts). The drama cries out for some strong dramatic music, and the whole key scheme of the opera (very carefully adhered to in each of the other scenes) demands a return to the key of the beginning of the act or its relative major (i.e. D, or F major). What is more, the contemporary printed libretto (a copy of which is preserved in the library of the Royal College of Music) has perfectly clear indications for a scene with the Sorceress and her Enchantresses, consisting of six lines of verse, and a dance to end the act. It is my considered opinion that music was certainly composed to this scene and has been lost. It is quite possible that it will be found, but each year makes it less likely.

'It is to me of prime importance dramatically as well as musically to include this missing scene, and so I have supplied other music of Purcell's to fit the six lines of the

[1]See 'Dido and Aeneas' by George Malcolm in *Benjamin Britten: a commentary* (edited by Mitchell and Keller).

libretto, and a dance to end in the appropriate key. . . .

'The realization of the figured bass for harpsichord is, of course, my own responsibility; in Purcell's time it was the custom for the keyboard player to work it out afresh at each performance. Therefore, no definitive version of this part is possible or desirable. . . .'

Dido and Aeneas was given in a dual bill with Monteverdi's *Combattimento di Tancredi e Clorinda* at the Lyric Theatre, Hammersmith, on May 1, 1951. Nancy Evans was Dido, and Joan Cross produced. Britten himself conducted from the harpsichord. After the Hammersmith season, it was played at the Aldeburgh, Holland, Cheltenham and Liverpool Festivals.

At the end of September, while engaged on the final stages of the orchestral score of *Billy Budd*, Britten, together with Peter Pears and a small group of friends, set out on a short cruise that took them direct from Aldeburgh, across the North Sea and up the Rhine as far as Bonn. While in Germany, Peter Pears sang the title part in *Oedipus Rex* in a performance for the Nordwestdeutscher Rundfunk, Cologne, that was conducted by Strawinsky, whose new opera, *The Rake's Progress*, had just been given at Venice.

Shortly after Britten's return, rehearsals started for *Billy Budd*. From discussion between the producer (Basil Coleman) and designer (John Piper), the general conclusion emerged that the sea and the ship would have to be suggested and not portrayed in realistic terms, and that the sets would have to be made 'so abstract that the absence or presence of particular details would not be noticed, so long as the shapes themselves were all intensely *ship-like*, and so long as the practical demands of the libretto and the score were all satisfied'.[1] This, on the whole, they succeeded in

---

[1] 'Billy Budd on the Stage' by Basil Coleman and John Piper. *Tempo*, Autumn, 1951.

doing—particularly in the scene on the berth-deck with its skeleton of wooden ribs, low headroom, swung hammocks and illusion of claustrophobia.

The first performance of *Billy Budd* took place at the Royal Opera House, Covent Garden, on December 1, 1951. Britten conducted; and the cast included Theodor Uppman in the title part, Peter Pears as Captain Vere and Frederick Dalberg as Claggart. Despite the possibility that the special nature of the subject and its all-male cast might restrict public interest, the first six performances were played to capacity houses. The opera was then taken on tour to Cardiff, Manchester, Glasgow and Birmingham; and when it returned to Covent Garden after Easter it continued to attract quite good attendances. In May the Covent Garden Opera Company gave two performances of it at the Théâtre des Champs-Elysées, Paris, during the Festival of Twentieth-Century Art. The attitude of the Parisian audience appears to have been rather tepid.

This was not so with the first German production at Wiesbaden in March 1952. Despite severe cuts that amounted almost to mutilations, the opera was an unqualified success with the public. The Earl of Harewood, who attended the sixth performance, wrote that the German audience's enthusiasm was something he could not 'remember ever having seen exceeded elsewhere'.[1]

True to his usual custom, Britten celebrated the completion of his new opera by composing a smaller-scale vocal work. The text of *Canticle II: Abraham and Isaac* is taken from the Chester Miracle Play and is set for alto, tenor and piano. The first performance was given by Kathleen Ferrier and Peter Pears at Nottingham (January 21, 1952) with the composer at the piano. The work is a dramatic scena, in which the tenor is cast as Abraham, the alto as Isaac; and

---

[1] 'Foreign Diary' by the Earl of Harewood. *Opera*, May 1952.

the two voices combine, whether in two parts or in unison, to form the voice of Jehovah. Just as the second String Quartet is an instrumental sequel to *Peter Grimes* this is a parergon to *Billy Budd*. It is a possible solution to the problem that confronts Captain Vere and Billy Budd; but in the opera the *deus ex machina* is absent. So far, the two *Canticles* are probably Britten's most beautiful and original vocal compositions.

Shortly after George VI's death in February 1952, Britten had the idea of writing an opera on the theme of Elizabeth I and Essex. This subject had made a strong impression on him when young; and when Her Majesty Elizabeth II gave him permission to compose an opera on the occasion of her Coronation, he received just the stimulus he needed. In the event, *Gloriana* was produced at a gala performance at the Royal Opera House, Covent Garden, on June 8, 1953, in the presence of the Queen and members of the Royal Family. It was an unique occasion. As Vaughan Williams pointed out in a letter to *The Times*,[1] this was 'the first time in history the Sovereign has commanded an opera by a composer from these islands for a great occasion'.

As his librettist, Britten chose William Plomer, with whom he had already had a number of discussions during the last few years with the idea of writing a new children's opera. Lytton Strachey's tragic history, *Elizabeth and Essex*, was the starting point of their collaboration; but, in the course of the opera's composition, both Plomer and Britten became 'less concerned than Strachey with the amatory motives of the two principal characters and more concerned with the Queen's pre-eminence as a Queen, a woman and a personality'.[2] The opera was planned so as to give considerable scope for pageantry—particularly the scenes of

---

[1] June 18, 1953.

[2] 'Notes on the Libretto of Gloriana' by William Plomer. *Tempo*, Summer, 1953.

the Masque at Norwich and the dancing at the Palace of Whitehall. Basil Coleman was the producer and John Piper the designer; and between them they devised a most magnificent and beautiful production, fully worthy of the great occasion for which the opera was written. John Pritchard conducted. Joan Cross was cast as Queen Elizabeth and gave one of the finest performances of her career. No one who was present at the gala performance will ever forget the extraordinary effect of Elizabeth I directly addressing the glittering audience grouped round Elizabeth II with the following words:

'I have ever used to set the last Judgment Day before mine eyes, and when I have to answer the highest Judge, I mean to plead that never thought was cherished in my heart that tended not to my people's good. I count it the glory of my crown that I have reigned with your love, and there is no jewel that I prefer before that jewel.'

Subsequent performances of *Gloriana* at Covent Garden drew nearly as full audiences as for *Billy Budd*; and its first performance outside London was given by the Covent Garden Opera Company at Bulawayo, Southern Rhodesia (August 8, 1953) at the Rhodes Centennial Exhibition.

CHAPTER VIII

Personal Postscript

Britten is first and foremost a professional musician. Composer, pianist, viola-player, conductor, research-scholar and musical editor—in the course of his career he has been engaged in multifarious activities connected with music, and if he has carried them out successfully and well, it is because he has taken the trouble to acquire the necessary technique. He has always believed in the importance of technique. In his broadcast talk *The Composer and the Listener* (1946) he said : 'Obviously it is no use having a technique unless you have the ideas to use this technique; but there is, unfortunately, a tendency in many quarters today to believe that brilliance of technique is a danger rather than a help. This is sheer nonsense. There has never been a composer worth his salt who has not had supreme technique. I'll go further than that and say that in the work of your supreme artist you can't separate inspiration from technique. I'd like anyone to tell me where Mozart's inspiration ends and technique begins.'

For technical reasons, among others, he is always prepared to work to order. He does not believe in allowing his talents to rust. As an artist he wants to serve the community and has shown himself ready to accept commissions of every kind. He finds virtue in serving all sorts of different persons and believes that even 'hackwork will not hurt an artist's integrity provided he does his best with every commission'.[1]

To have as many new ideas as he has and to work as hard as he does argues not only extraordinary fertility and fluency but also great sensitivity. If an artist lacks feeling,

---

[1]Quoted in 'Benjamin Britten: Another Purcell' by Phoebe Douglas. *Town & Country*, December 1947.

he loses much of the impetus towards expression. Britten shows himself sensitive in many ways—particularly to cruelty and suffering. Many of his operas contain (or imply) scenes of almost sadistic cruelty, but they inevitably lead to episodes of warm compassion and pity. This intense sympathy with the victims of oppression probably lies at the basis of his pacifism; and Hans Keller has made the interesting suggestion[1] that 'by dint of character, musical history and environment, he has become a *musical pacifist* too'.

He is also sensitive to critical misunderstanding, or lack of understanding, especially where it appears to be the result of wilfulness or stupidity.[2] In his own case, it is not as if his music were particularly obscure or revolutionary. His style is eclectic; his idiom modal; his musical metrics often echo the more or less familiar structure of English poetical metrics. The surface value of his music is quite easy to understand: but an appreciation merely of its superficial qualities is not going to reach the heart of the matter.

As an occasional composer he has a flair for the various elements that make an occasion unique, and his works are often supremely effective in the setting and circumstances for which they were designed. It is this feeling for what is likely 'to come off' in performance that has stood him in such good stead in his music for opera-house, theatre, cinema and radio.

Furthermore, he has always shown himself extremely sensitive to the relationship of words and music. He is not inhibited about words like some composers; but he justly assesses the different values of the syllable, the word, and the idea behind the word, and knows how to give them a

---

[1] 'The Musical Character' by Hans Keller. *Benjamin Britten: a commentary*.

[2] See 'Variations on a Critical Theme' by Benjamin Britten. *Opera*, March 1952.

musical gravity of their own. Sometimes one has the f[
that his instrumental music aspires to the condition of
or choral music; and sometimes in the vocal and choral
music one has the feeling that the word has been made
music and the music has taken on a new dimension. If
critics object that the issue is being confused by the presence of an extra-musical element, the answer must be that
precisely this combination of disparate elements lies at the
heart of the problem of opera, and Britten has approached
excitingly near to one of the possible solutions.

Occasionally the effect on listeners is so overwhelming
that normal critical standards seem to be swept away.
E. M. Forster's comment on the first performance of *Saint
Nicolas* at Aldeburgh has already been quoted—'It was one
of those triumphs outside the rules of art which only the
great artist can achieve.' The same work had a very similar
effect on another critic. Donald Mitchell wrote:[1] 'I was so
confused by its progressively overwhelming impact that all
I could find to say was: "This is too beautiful".' Perhaps
Auden in his poem *The Composer*[2] has found the best way
of putting into words the inexplicable thrill that floods the
mind and senses at such a moment.

> *Pour out your presence, O delight, cascading*
> *The falls of the knee and the weirs of the spine,*
> *Our climate of silence and doubt invading;*
> *You alone, alone, O imaginary song,*
> *Are unable to say an existence is wrong,*
> *And pour out your forgiveness like a wine.*

There are many aspects of Britten's character that could
be pursued if one felt inclined. His sense of humour (or
should one say his sense of proportion?); his brisk fancy

---

[1] 'A Note on Saint Nicolas: Some Points of Britten's Style' by Donald
Mitchell. *Music Survey*, Spring, 1950.
[2] *Another Time*, XXII.

and ambivalent imagination; his fondness for children. He remembers with pleasure his own youth in East Anglia—fêtes and obstacle races, bicycle rides, tennis tournaments, bathing parties, making friends and making music—and projects himself without difficulty into the minds and hearts of young people today. That is why he writes such good music about children and for them to listen to and play.

Although his success has naturally excited a certain measure of opposition and jealousy, his career has not gone unhonoured.

Suffolk is his home county. He was born there, and he lives there today. Some of his operas are set there—*Peter Grimes*, *Albert Herring* and *The Little Sweep*. It was therefore a fine compliment when in the summer of 1951 he was made an Honorary Freeman of the Borough of Lowestoft. On that occasion he took the opportunity of confirming his allegiance to that part of England. In his speech of thanks he said: 'Suffolk, the birthplace and inspiration of Constable and Gainsborough, the loveliest of English painters; the home of Crabbe, that most English of poets; Suffolk, with its rolling, intimate countryside; its heavenly Gothic churches, big and small; its marshes, with those wild sea-birds; its grand ports and its little fishing villages. I am firmly rooted in this glorious county. And I proved this to myself when I once tried to live somewhere else.'

His services to English music have been outstanding; and it is partly due to him that today it is better known and stands higher in the esteem of countries abroad than was ever the case before. It was a well deserved tribute, therefore, when he was created a Companion of Honour in the Coronation Honours of 1953.

PART TWO
The Operas

CHAPTER I

Paul Bunyan

At the time of its first performance *Paul Bunyan* was described by its authors as a choral operetta with many small parts rather than a few star roles.

For his subject Auden took the legend of Paul Bunyan. This giant lumberman, together with his various friends and Babe the Blue Ox, who was reputed to stand forty-two axe handles high and to sport a twist of chewing tobacco between his horns, was among the pioneers working in the American wilderness who helped prepare the way for the advance of civilization westwards. Auden considered America to be unique in being the only country to create myths after the industrial revolution, and this particular legend to be not only American but universal in its implications. He looked on Paul Bunyan as 'a projection of the collective state of mind of a people whose tasks were primarily the physical mastery of nature'[1] and intended that the operetta should present 'in a compressed fairy-story form the development of the continent from a virgin forest before the birth of Paul Bunyan to settlement and cultivation when Paul Bunyan says goodbye because he is no longer needed'.[1] He included a number of Bunyan's friends, including Hel Helson, his brawny Swedish foreman, and Johnny Inkslinger, his intelligent bookkeeper, but omitted Babe the Blue Ox, whom he interpreted as being a symbol of Bunyan's anima.

In view of his previous record as poet and playright, he was hardly likely to approach his subject from a literal or realistic angle; and it is not surprising that he tried to surmount the three main difficulties confronting him in ways

---

[1]Quotations from the *Paul Bunyan* programme.

consistent with the didactic style of epic drama as advocated by Brecht.

'In the first place', as he explained,[1] '[Bunyan's] size and general mythical characteristics prevent his physical appearance on the stage—he is presented as a voice and, in order to differentiate him from the human characters, as a speaking voice. In consequence some one else had to be found to play the chief dramatic role, and Inkslinger seemed the most suitable, as satisfying Henry James's plea for a fine lucid intelligence as a compositional centre. Inkslinger, in fact, is the only person capable of understanding who Paul Bunyan really is, and, in a sense, the operetta is an account of his process of discovery. In the second place, the theatrical presentation of the majority of Bunyan's exploits would require the resources of Bayreuth, but not to refer to them at all would leave his character all too vaguely in the air. To get round this difficulty we have interposed simple narrative ballads between the scenes, as it were, as solo Greek chorus. Lastly, an opera with no female voices, would be hard to produce and harder to listen to, yet in its earlier stages at least the conversion of forests into lumber is an exclusively male occupation. Accordingly we have introduced *a camp dog* and *two camp cats* sung by a coloratura soprano and two mezzo-sopranos respectively.'

In view of Britten's later career as an opera composer, there are several points of special interest here. In the first place, the focussing on Inkslinger as a 'compositional centre' because of his intelligence and understanding of the real nature of Bunyan is paralleled in *Billy Budd* by the way the true significance of Budd's tragedy is perceived and revealed by Captain Vere. Secondly, the 'solo Greek chorus' is also met with in *The Rape of Lucretia*, where Britten and Duncan took over this device from Obey's play *Le Viol de*

---

[1]'Opera on an American Legend' by W. H. Auden, *New York Times*, May 4, 1941.

Lucrèce. Thirdly, in *Billy Budd*, Britten and his librettists had the courage to write an opera with an all-male cast, and it was produced with conspicuous success.

Neither the libretto nor the score of *Paul Bunyan* has ever been published—in fact, so many changes to text and music were made in the green room at the Brander Matthews Hall, Columbia University, during the operetta's run that no definitive version can be said to exist. Accordingly, it may be of interest to give brief details of the production, characters and scene as set out in the original programme, and a few excerpts from the press reviews.

Paul Bunyan was presented on May 5, 1941, for a week's run by the Columbia Theater Associates of Columbia University, with the co-operation of the Columbia University Department of Music and a chorus from the New York Schola Cantorum. It was financed by a grant from the Alice M. Ditson Fund. The producer was Milton Smith, and the conductor Hugh Ross.

CHARACTERS

In the Prologue
Old Trees   Young Trees   Three Wild Geese

In the Interludes   Narrator

In the Play   The Voice of Paul Bunyan
Cross Crosshaulson   John Shears   Sam Sharkey
Ben Benny   Jen Jenson   Pete Peterson
            Andy Anderson   Other Lumberjacks
Western Union Boy   Hel Helson   Johnny Inkslinger
*Fido   *Moppet   *Poppet
                          The Defeated
Slim   Tiny
                    The Film Stars and Models
                          Frontier Women

Scene: A Grove in a Western Forest
            Prologue   —   Night
            Act I   Scene 1   —   A Spring Morning
                     Scene 2   —   Summer
            Act II   Scene 1   —   Autumn
                     Scene 2   —   Christmas

* These are the camp dog and two camp cats mentioned above.

On the whole the work was received by the New York critics with dismay. *Time*, suspicious of this 'anemic operetta put up by two British expatriates', complained that it 'was as bewildering and irritating a treatment of the outsize lumberman as any two Englishmen could have devised'. *The New Yorker* said that though on paper or in conference there may have been certain items that 'looked like the makings of something pretty exciting . . . in the theatre *Paul Bunyan* didn't jell'. Virgil Thomson in the *New York Herald Tribune* attacked the form of the work. He decided it fell into the category 'of the Auden semi-poetic play' and went on to state that 'on the stage [the Auden style] has always been a flop. . . . Every sentence is indirect and therefore unsuited to musical declamation. Every dramatic moment has the afflatus taken out of it before the composer can get it over to the audience'.

Of the composer Virgil Thomson wrote: 'Mr. Britten's work in *Paul Bunyan* is sort of witty at its best. Otherwise it is undistinguished.' A more revealing description of the music came from Robert Bagar in *World Telegraph*. 'Mr. Britten, who is an up and coming composer, has written some worth-while tunes in this score. It ranges, in passing, from part writing to single jingle. Its rhythms are often interesting and the harmonies fit rather well. There are arias, recitatives, small ensembles and big choral sequences. Most of the last named are good. The music makes occasional reference to *Cavalleria Rusticana* and one item, a stuttering bit,[1] goes back to *The Bartered Bride*.' Other critics were reminded of Rossini, Gilbert and Sullivan, Rimsky-Korsakoff, Prokofieff, Shostakovich and Marc Blitzstein's *The Cradle Will Rock*.

But the most important review came from Olin Downes in the *New York Times*. Although he had a number of reservations to make, he admitted that Britten 'knows how

---

[1]Another anticipation of *Billy Budd*.

to set a text, how to orchestrate in an economical and telling fashion, how to underscore dialogue with orchestral commentary'. He added: 'What is done by Mr. Britten shows more clearly than ever that opera written for a small stage, with relatively modest forces for the presentation, in the English language, and in ways pleasantly free from the stiff tradition of either grand or light opera of the past, is not only a possibility but a development nearly upon us.'

His words were to prove prophetic. Far from being discouraged by the reception of *Paul Bunyan*, Britten forged ahead with his plans for *Peter Grimes*, and only five years were to elapse before the production of his first chamber opera, *The Rape of Lucretia*. As for Auden, he waited longer and, in 1948, in collaboration with Chester Kallman, provided Strawinsky with the libretto for *The Rake's Progress*.

CHAPTER II

Peter Grimes

I

When Britten approached Montagu Slater in 1942 and asked him to write a libretto for the opera that had been commissioned by the Koussevitzky Music Foundation, the theme was already fixed—Aldeburgh was to be the scene and the subject Peter Grimes, the story of whose life is told by Crabbe in *The Borough*.

Aldeburgh was Crabbe's birthplace, He was born there on January 1, 1755. His son described it as a poor and wretched place lying between 'a low hill or cliff, on which only the old church and a few better houses were then situated, and the beach of the German Ocean. It consisted of two parallel and unpaved streets, running between mean and scrambling houses, the abodes of seafaring men, pilots and fishers. The range of houses nearest to the sea had suffered so much from repeated invasions of the waves, that only a few scattered tenements appeared erect among the desolation'.[1] As for the beach, then as now it consisted of 'large rolled stones, then loose shingle, and, at the fall of the tide, a stripe of fine hard sand. Vessels of all sorts, from the large heavy troll-boat to the yawl and prame, drawn up along the shore—fishermen preparing their tackle, or sorting their spoil—and, nearer the gloomy old town-hall (the only indication of municipal dignity) a few groups of mariners, chiefly pilots, taking their quick, short walk backwards and forwards, every eye watchful of a signal from the offing—such was the squalid scene that first opened on the author of *The Village*'. And such was the place and community that in 1810 Crabbe described so vividly in his poem

[1] *The Life of George Crabbe, by his Son,* 1834.

The Borough by means of a series of twenty-four letters written in heroic couplets.

In the first of these letters, he gives a general description of the Borough. He mentions the River Alde, which (as his son explains) 'approaches the sea close to Aldeburgh, within a few hundred yards, and then turning abruptly continues to run for about ten miles parallel to the beach, until it at length finds its embouchure at Orford'; the craft on the river—'hoys, pinks and sloops; brigs, brigantines and snows'—and also the quayside with its clamour of sailors and carters and lumber of 'package and parcel, hogshead, chest, and case'. After night-fall some of the inhabitants of the Borough pass their times at parties, whist-drives, concerts, plays or taverns, while—

> *Others advent'rous walk abroad and meet*
> *Returning Parties pacing through the Street . . .*
> *When Tavern-Lights flit on from Room to Room,*
> *And guide the tippling Sailor staggering home;*
> *There as we pass the jingling Bells betray,*
> *How Business rises with the closing Day;*
> *Now walking silent, by the River's side,*
> *The Ear perceives the rimpling of the Tide;*
> *Or measur'd cadence of the Lads who tow*
> *Some enter'd Hoy, to fix her in her row;*
> *Or hollow sound, which from the Parish-Bell,*
> *To some departed Spirit bids farewell!*

Crabbe then proceeds to deal with the various professions and trades in the Borough. Letter XI enumerates the inns—particularly *The Boar*.

> *There dwells a kind old Aunt, and there you see*
> *Some kind young Nieces in her company;*
> *Poor village Nieces, whom the tender Dame*
> *Invites to Town, and gives their Beauty fame.*

No fewer than ten of the later letters are devoted to the inhabitants of the almshouse and to the poor; and among the latter figure Abel Keene, a clerk in office (Letter XXI), Ellen Orford, the widowed schoolmistress (Letter XX), and Peter Grimes, a fisherman (Letter XXII). From the first, Slater borrowed no more than his surname, which he attached to Ned, the quack (who is described in Letter VII); the second he elevated to the principal female part; and the third became the protagonist of the opera.

Edward Fitzgerald, who was a friend of Crabbe's son, has left it on record that the Peter Grimes of the poem was based on an actual fisherman named Tom Brown, who lived in Aldeburgh in the middle of the 18th century. According to Crabbe, there were few redeeming features about Peter Grimes. As soon as he was out of his teens, he became impatient of parental control and started to knock his father about. Then he went to live on his own and 'fished by water and filched by land'; but he was dissatisfied so long as there was no unfortunate victim living with him on whom he could wreak his strength at any hour of the day or night. Presently he heard of workhouse-clearing men in London who were prepared to bind orphan parish-boys to needy tradesmen. He obtained such an apprentice for himself and was at last able to give full rein to his sadistic instincts and his lust for power. The first apprentice, Sam, lived for three years and then was found lifeless in his bed. The second fell one night from the main-mast of the fishing boat and was killed. The third died in the course of a stormy voyage from Aldeburgh to London. After his death, the conscience of the Borough was thoroughly roused; and the Mayor himself forbad Grimes to take any more apprentices to work with him. Thenceforward he was ostracized. Gradually his mind began to fail and, as he sailed up and down the river, he was haunted by the spirits of his father and two of the dead boys. In raving delirium shortly before his death he described one such scene:

In one fierce Summer-day, when my poor Brain
Was burning-hot and cruel was my Pain,
Then came this Father-foe, and there he stood
With his two Boys again upon the Flood;
There was more Mischief in their Eyes, more Glee
In their pale Faces when they glar'd at me;
Still did they force me on the Oar to rest,
And when they saw me fainting and opprest,
He, with his Hand, the old Man, scoop'd the Flood,
And there came Flame about him mix'd with Blood;
He bade me stoop and look upon the place,
Then flung the hot-red Liquor in my Face;
Burning it blaz'd, and then I roar'd for Pain,
I thought the Daemons would have turn'd my Brain.

In the Preface to *The Borough*, Crabbe embarks on a brief analysis of the character of Peter Grimes. 'The mind here exhibited', he says, 'is one untouched by pity, unstung by remorse, and uncorrected by shame: yet is this hardihood of temper and spirit broken by want, disease, solitude and disappointment; and he becomes the victim of a distempered and horror-stricken fancy. . . . The corrosion of hopeless want, the wasting of unabating disease, and the gloom of unvaried solitude, will have their effect on every nature; and the harder that nature is, and the longer time required to work upon it, so much the more strong and indelible is the impression.'

If Peter Grimes was to become the hero of a twentieth century opera and win the sympathy of a modern audience, some of these eighteenth century values would have to be altered and adjusted. Slater accordingly embarked on a reinterpretation of the character, as a result of which Crabbe's grim fisherman became something of a Borough Byron, too proud and self-willed to come to terms with society, and yet sufficiently imaginative to be fully conscious of his loss. A clue to this new reading is perhaps to be found in an episode of Grimes's childhood, which becomes even more poignant when it is remembered that Crabbe too as a boy had been bitterly hostile to his own father. Grimes recalled

> *How, when the Father in his Bible read,*
> *He in contempt and anger left the Shed;*
> *'It is the Word of Life', the Parent cried;*
> *—'This is the Life itself', the Boy replied.*

To fit his more modern interpretation, Slater decided to post-date the action of the drama from the latter part of the eighteenth century when the stories related in *The Borough* actually took place, to 1830 when the tide of Byronism was in full flood. In view of the usual time-lag between metropolitan and provincial fashions, little or no injury was thereby done to the accuracy of the general description of the Borough and its inhabitants as based on Crabbe; but the new date accentuated the rift between Grimes and the rest of the community—between, on the one hand, the comparatively modern type of the psychopathic introvert, divided against himself and against the world, and, on the other, reactionary extrovert society.

For the purpose of his plot, Slater omitted Peter's father and reduced the number of his apprentices from three to two, the first of whom has just died at sea when the opera opens. Ellen Orford, the widowed schoolmistress, is promoted to the position of Peter's friend and confidante—in fact, there is a moment when Peter deludes himself into thinking his problems would be solved if he could marry her. At the end of the inquest into the apprentice's death, Ellen asks Peter to come away with her; but he feels he cannot accept until he has rehabilitated himself in the eyes of the Borough—and to him rehabilitation means money, wealth. He explains this to Captain Balstrode, a retired sea-captain, during the storm in Act I:

These Borough gossips
Listen to money,
Only to money.
I'll fish the sea dry,
Sell the good catches.
That wealthy merchant
Grimes will set up
Household and shop.
You will all see it!
I'll marry Ellen!

Balstrode replies:

Man—go and ask her,
Without your booty,
She'll have you now.

But when Peter demurs at the idea of being accepted out of pity, Balstrode realizes that it is too late to remedy the defects in his character and that sooner or later the fatal pattern of the former tragedy is bound to be repeated. And so it turns out. The new apprentice arrives; but although he is ill-treated by Peter, it is accident rather than deliberate cruelty that ultimately brings about his death. By then, however, the Borough conscience has been thoroughly aroused—the man-hunt is up—and Balstrode realizes that the best thing for Peter will be to disappear. But how? At an earlier point in the action, Peter, asked why he didn't leave the Borough to 'try the wider sea with merchantman or privateer', replied:

I am native, rooted here ...
By familiar fields,
Marsh and sand,
Ordinary streets,
Prevailing wind.

As exile is out of the question, the only alternative appears to be suicide; and on Balstrode's advice, he sails his fishing boat out to sea and scuttles it.

Through his imagination Peter is aware of wider universal issues at stake at the same time as he wrestles with the immediate problems caused by the flaws in his nature. This is made clear from his soliloquy in the crowded pub during the storm in Act I:

> *Now the Great Bear and Pleiades*
> > *where earth moves*
> *Are drawing up the clouds*
> > *of human grief*
> *Breathing solemnity in the deep night.*
> *But if the horoscope's*
> > *bewildering . . .*
> *Who can turn the skies back and begin again?*

And this intensity of vision helps to raise to the tragic plane what might otherwise have been merely a sordid drama of realism.

Here is a synopsis of the libretto:

Prologue. The interior of the Moot Hall. At the end of the inquest into the death of Peter Grimes's apprentice, Mr. Swallow, the coroner, brings in a verdict of death in accidental circumstances; but Peter complains that this verdict does not really clear him of the charge, for the case will still go on in people's minds.   *Act I, Scene i.* A street by the sea a few days later, showing the exterior of the Moot Hall and *The Boar*. Peter is already experiencing difficulty in working his fishing boat single-handed; but Ned Keene, the apothecary, tells him he has found another apprentice boy, whom Ellen Orford, despite the general disapproval of the Borough, agrees to fetch by the carrier's cart. Shortly after her departure, a storm breaks, which is all the more to be feared because it comes with a spring tide. The boats are made fast, the nets brought in and the windows of the houses shuttered. After a dialogue between Peter and Captain Balstrode, the scene changes to *The Boar* (*Act I, Scene ii*) on the evening of the same day. Although it is past closing time, the pub is full, and people are still coming in out of the storm for shelter and refreshment. News is brought that the coast road has been flooded and a landslide has swept away part of the cliff up by Peter Grimes's hut. A quarrel or two break out among the topers; a round is sung; and when at last Ellen Orford arrives back with the boy, Peter—to everyone's consternation—insists on taking him away at once to his desolate hut.

Act II, Scene i. The scene is the same as in Act I, Scene i; the time a Sunday morning a few weeks later. Ellen and Peter's new apprentice sit in the sun on the beach, while morning service goes on in the Parish Church. By chance she discovers the boy's clothes are torn and his body bruised; and when Peter, who has just caught sight of a shoal, arrives to take him out fishing, her reproaches lead to an open quarrel between the two, which is overseen and overheard by some of the neighbours. By the time the church service is over, the news has spread round the Borough that '*Grimes is at his exercise!*' and a party of men sets out to investigate. Meanwhile, Peter and the apprentice have reached his hut, which is made out of an old upturned boat (*Act II, Scene ii*). Here he gathers together his fishing gear; but the boy's blubbering delays him and when, after a clumsy attempt to soothe the lad, he hears the sound of the neighbours coming up the hill, he suddenly decides to make a quick get-away. He flings his nets and tackle out of the cliff-side door; but the boy, as he starts to climb down the cliff, slips and is dashed to death. Peter scrambles down after him. On arrival, the search party—to its surprise—finds the hut empty, neatly kept and reasonably clean.

Act III, Scene i. The scene is the same as in the first scenes of Acts I and II; the time, two or three nights later. A subscription dance is taking place in the Moot Hall, and there is considerable traffic between the Hall and *The Boar*. Though neither Peter nor his apprentice has been seen during the last few days, it is assumed that both are away fishing, until Mrs. Sedley, one of the leading gossips in the Borough with a keen nose for scenting out crime as well as scandal, overhears Ellen telling Balstrode that the jersey she embroidered for the boy has been found washed up on the beach. Seeing that Peter's boat is now back in harbour, she imparts her suspicions to Swallow, who in his capacity as Mayor summons the constable of the Borough and bids him take a posse of men to apprehend Grimes. A few hours later (*Act III, Scene ii*) the dance in the Moot Hall is over, a fog has crept up from the sea, and only the occasional cries of the man-hunt and the moan of a fog-horn break the stillness of the night, as Peter creeps back to his boat. This is where Ellen and Balstrode find him, hungry, wet, exhausted, almost insane. It is Balstrode who proposes the way out—that he take his boat out to sea, scuttle it and sink with it—and this Peter does, as dawn breaks. Gradually the Borough awakes to life. Lights appear at windows. Shutters are drawn back. The coastguard station reports a boat sinking far out at sea, but the news is dismissed as an idle rumour; and as the light of the morning waxes, the people of the Borough start to go about their daily tasks. It is the beginning of another day.

This outline is sufficient to show how far Slater's libretto is removed from Crabbe and *The Borough*, and how fundamentally different a character Slater's Grimes is from Crabbe's. Slater himself has explained that 'the story as worked out in the opera uses Crabbe's poem only as a starting-point. Crabbe produced character sketches of some of the main persons of the drama. I have taken these character sketches as clues and woven them into a story against the background of the Borough: but it is my story and the composer's (the idea was originally not mine but Britten's), and I have to take the responsibility for its shape as well as its words'.[1]

In writing his libretto, Slater avoided the heroic couplet as used by Crabbe and blank verse, because he felt that the five-stress line was 'out of key with contemporary modes of thought and speech'.[2] Instead, he adopted a 'four-stress line with rough rhymes for the body of the drama', while the Prologue was written in prose and various metres used for the set numbers.

II

When Britten started to set this libretto, he was confronted by various problems.

In the first place, the division of each of the three acts of the opera into two scenes, the action of which was continuous or nearly continuous or partly overlapping, made it possible for him to decide to compose each act as an unbroken piece of music; but as there were scene changes between scenes i and ii of Acts I and II, interludes would be needed there, and a further interlude of some sort was indicated between scenes i and ii of Act III to mark the passing of time. There was also the formal problem of the Prologue to consider. Prosaic though it might be, it gave such back history as was needed, provided an exposition of the theme and introduced the main characters of the opera by name—all this so expeditiously and succinctly that it could hardly be expected to stand alone. Clearly, it ought to be joined to Act I; and this would entail another

---

[1] *Peter Grimes: Sadler's Well's Opera Books No. 3*, edited by Eric Crozier. The Bodley Head, 1945.

[2] *Peter Grimes and Other Poems* by Montagu Slater. The Bodley Head' 1946.

interlude to cover the necessary scene change. To complete the scheme, he added introductions to Acts II and III, making a total of six orchestral 'interludes' in all.

And then he had also to take into account the fact that each act of Slater's libretto contained cues for actual sound or song effects as opposed to the music to be composed in accordance with operatic convention. For instance: The scene in *The Boar* works up to a moment when a song is suggested and someone spontaneously starts up a round, '*Old Joe has gone fishing*', in which the rest of the company joins. The following Act opens with Ellen talking to the boy apprentice on the beach, while from the neighbouring church are overheard strains of the Sunday morning service. Later that morning, some of the men of the Borough form a procession and, led by Hobson the carter playing a tenor drum, go off to Peter's hut, chanting a sinister marching song. In the last Act, the dance band at the Moot Hall, consisting of fiddle, double-bass, two clarinets and percussion, is heard playing fragments of a barn dance, waltz *alla Ländler*, hornpipe and galop. And later that night, when the man-hunt is up, the search for Grimes is punctuated by the slow booming of a fog-horn.

In the scene in *The Boar*, not only was it important for the round to stand out properly in its context; but there was the added complication of storm without and warmth and drink-happy company within. Here he profited by his experience in writing for radio drama. The technique of the mixing panel had shown him how varied were the possibilities of using music at different levels—background, foreground or intermediate—and how with two or more distinct streams of sound, one could be brought up into the foreground while the other was faded out, or (if necessary) the two streams could be mixed together. He accordingly decided to depict the storm in its full fury in Interlude II and shut it out as soon as the curtain went up. Most of the

scene in *The Boar* is accordingly set to an animated form of
free recitative, punctuated by brief fragments of the storm
that burst through the doorway as various characters enter
from outside; and this provides an excellent setting for the
round. Thanks to the cross-fading device, the music of the
storm, having been heard in full in Interlude II, continues
by implication unbrokenly throughout this scene.

Cross-fading is also used for the church service, the song
chanted by the procession that visits Peter's hut, and the
Moot Hall dance.

As for the fog-horn, Britten realized that here was an
unique opportunity for dramatic effect. As the first half of
the second scene of Act III is virtually a soliloquy by
Grimes, let the orchestra be silent after the *fortissimo*
shouts of the chorus at the end of the previous scene and let
Grimes's monologue be accompanied only by the fog-horn
and occasional cries from the distant man-hunt. Then when
he has sailed out to sea to drown himself and life returns to
the Borough with the dawn of another day, the repetition
of the orchestral music from the opening of Act I will be
particularly impressive.

The first Interlude, joining the Prologue to Act I, is based
on three motifs.

Ex. 1
Lento e tranquillo

(*a*) The high unison strings that faintly outline the key of A
minor cling hard and long to each holding note, and the
tension is emphasized by the grace notes; (*b*) in the middle

register, *arpeggi* of diatonic thirds from the harp reinforced by clarinets and violas, describe fragmentary arcs of sound; and this musical superstructure is underpinned by (*c*) a sequence of slowly shifting bass chords from the brass—A major against the shrill A minor of the upper strings. It is not over-fanciful to find these three motifs evocative of (*a*) the wind that 'is holding back the tide', as it blows through the rigging of the boats on the beach and over the chimney-pots of the Borough, (*b*) the lapping of the water, and (*c*) the scrunch of the shingle beneath the tide. The clash between major and minor gives an extraordinarily salty tang to the scene.

Interlude II is a storm piece of almost symphonic stature, which might take the following lines of Crabbe as motto:

> But nearer Land you may the Billows trace,
> As if contending in their watery chace . . .
> Curl'd as they come, they strike with furious force,
> And then re-flowing, take their grating course,
> Raking the rounded Flints, which ages past
> Roll'd by their rage, and shall to ages last.

It follows directly on the unresolved cadence of Peter's monologue at the end of Act I, Scene i, and its four main episodes are: (*a*) a theme (*presto con fuoco*), which is treated fugally at its first appearance, and whose periodic recurrence in different forms gives this Interlude something of the character of a rondo; (*b*) an altered form of the brass groundswell theme from the first Interlude, with a particularly grinding passage of close imitation at the interval of a minor ninth; (*c*) a grotesque bitonal passage in triplets (*molto animato*), where the gale indulges in particularly malicious pranks in the keys of D natural and E flat simultaneously; and (*d*) a reprise and development of the music of Peter's unresolved monologue from the end of the previous scene.

This Interlude is broken off short by the rise of the curtain on the scene in the interior of *The Boar;* but, as explained above, its continuance is implicit in the fragmentary bits of storm that burst into the pub each time someone opens the door. These make it clear that the episodes of the storm Interlude are following each other in the same order as above; but when a strangely altered phrase from (*d*) ushers in Peter's arrival, it serves as direct introduction to his soliloquy, '*Now the Great Bear and Pleiades*', which is thereby given a wider, more universal significance.

The third Interlude is an impressionist description of the sea on a warm sunny Sunday morning—the greatest possible contrast to the storm of the previous Act (A major after E flat minor). An *ostinato* by the horns playing contiguous but overlapping thirds gives a kind of blurred background to a merry toccata-like theme for woodwind. This

Ex. 2

with the syncopated reiteration of its notes recalls the animated glitter of sunlight on water. After a brief episode consisting of a sustained tune from cellos and violas rising and then falling back through an octave, the toccata material is repeated and leads directly to the rise of the curtain and Ellen's opening *arioso*, '*Glitter of waves and glitter of sunlight*', which is set to the tune from the preceding episode, but now appearing a fourth higher and in the key of D.

As in Shostakovich's *Lady Macbeth of Mtsensk*, the central Interlude is a passacaglia. The turning-point of the opera has been reached in the middle of Act II, Scene i, when, after striking Ellen at the end of their quarrel, Peter is overcome by the full realization of their failure and cries out *'God have mercy upon me!'* The musical phrase to which these words are sung becomes a key motif for the

rest of the opera. After providing the main theme of the following chorus, *'Grimes is at his exercise!'* it serves (in

augmented form) as the ground-bass of the passacaglia and later will be found inverted.

This passacaglia Interlude, in which it may be said that Peter's apprentice who has been mute throughout the opera at last becomes musically articulate, consists of an air for solo viola

followed by nine variations, all of them developed freely over this unchanging ground-bass (key of F). The last variation, a fugal *stretto*, leads directly into the next scene, which opens with a series of disjointed ejaculations from

Peter, punctuated by scrappy orchestral references to eight of the foregoing variations. In this way, Britten makes it clear that just as Interlude II depicted the fury of the storm as it impinged on the senses, so Interlude IV reflects the agony that is undermining Peter's mind. The true close of the passacaglia is deferred until the end of Act II, just after the apprentice's death. Then, through a whispering *bisbigliando* figure for celesta, the solo viola repeats the original

air inverted, at the end of which the ground bass returns for a single final statement (key of C).

The two remaining Interludes are not so fully developed from the musical point of view. Like those introducing Acts I and II, Interlude V is a descriptive piece. By skilful placing, a sequence of almost static swell chords (mainly in their first and second inversions), strung together on a thread of quietly-moving inner parts, is made to suggest the tranquil beauty of the sea and Borough under the moon. A secondary theme played by flutes and harp, which gives the impression of an occasional glint of reflected moonlight from wave or slaty roof or weather-cock, should be contrasted with the gayer and more glittering daylight toccata theme of Interlude III.

The last Interlude is a cadenza freely improvised by various instruments over, under and through a ghostlike chord of the dominant. This chord arises like a faint overtone between the mighty shouts of '*Peter Grimes!*' at the end of the previous scene, is sustained by the muted horns pianissimo throughout the movement, and at the beginning of the last scene melts into the distant voices (off) still shouting *'Grimes!'* The effect of this ostinato is to emphaszie the all-pervasive featureless fog, while the free improvization of the orchestra, based on snatches of many previous themes, shows something of the raging turbulence and agony of Peter's mind.

The main purpose of these Interludes is to serve as impressionist and expressionist introductions to the realistic scenes of the opera, in much the same way as Virginia Woolf used the device of prose poems about the sea to introduce each different section and period of her novel *The Waves*, and also to secure continuity within the acts.

As for vocal presentation, Britten decided (in his own words) to embrace 'the classical practice of separate numbers that crystallize and hold the emotion of a dramatic situation at chosen moments'.[1] He did not, however, make each number complete and self-contained, but by following a method of construction similar to that used (for instance) by Verdi in *Falstaff* succeeded in reconciling the classical practice of separate numbers with an uninterrupted musical action. *Peter Grimes* is the first of his operas that shows with what remarkable skill he manages the transitions between the various degrees of intensity needed for recitatives, airs, *ariosi* and concerted numbers, and how he usually allows the emotion engendered by each number to lead on to its sequel before the musical construction can reach a full close. The music flows accordingly without check or hiatus from the beginning to the end of each act, and this continuity of development is achieved at the expense of any sense of interim relaxation.

The nearest approach to the fully developed air is to be found in Ellen's solos in Acts I and III: '*Let her among you without fault cast the first stone*' and '*Embroidery in childhood was a luxury of idleness*'. Her song in Act II, '*We*

---

[1] *Peter Grimes: Sadler's Wells Opera Books No. 3.*

planned that their lives should have a new start', would fall into this category too, were it not for the fact that it excites the comments and interruptions of so many bystanders that after a few bars it becomes an eleven-part concerted ensemble and then the full chorus joins in.

As for Peter, his solos are in the nature of monologues or soliloquies; and their construction is looser and more rhapsodic accordingly. It has already been shown how his solo at the end of Act I, Scene i is at first interrupted and then resumed by the storm Interlude, and how it is (as it were) completed by his soliloquy, *'Now the Great Bear and Pleiades'*, in the middle of the subsequent scene. It may also be argued that his air in the hut, *'And she will soon forget her schoolhouse ways'*, is a further instalment from the same large utterance, for it shows its strong family likeness to the earlier passages by its diatonic idiom and its consistent loyalty to the tonality of sharp keys (e.g., A and E).

There is one other fully developed musical number that deserves special mention, and that is the impassive quartet of women's voices that occurs at the end of Act II, Scene i and forms such an excellent contrast to the all-male vocal writing of the following scene. When the procession of men has marched off to Peter's hut, Ellen, Auntie (the proprietress of *The Boar*) and her two nieces remain behind and dejectedly reflect on women's lot. A *ritornello* of bedraggled trailing diatonic seconds played by the flutes separates each phrase of this trio, and the vocal parts, which are generally a major second lower than the notes of the accompaniment, betray a sluttish weariness—which conforms well with the character of Auntie and her nieces.

Most of the minor characters have an opportunity of singing memorable phrases of song, generally in stanza form and sometimes with a refrain, and these can perhaps best be described as half-numbers. Such are Hobson's song (Act I, Scene i), *'I have to go from pub to pub'*, in which the second verse is sung by Ellen; Auntie's song (I, ii) with its refrain '*A joke's a joke and fun is fun*'; Balstrode's song in the same scene, '*Pub conversation should depend*' with its refrain '*We live and let live and look we keep our hands to ourselves!*'; and in Act III, Scene i Swallow's tipsy '*Assign your prettiness to me*' and the Rector's goodnight '*I'll water my roses*' with its male-voice sextet accompaniment. In addition, there is the capstan shanty in Act I, Scene i, '*I'll give a hand*', which is started up by Balstrode, who is subsequently joined by Keene as helper and Auntie and Bob Boles, the Methodist fisherman, as lookers-on.

Stimulated but also kept on tenterhooks by these half-measures, the listener longs for the satisfaction of a fully completed musical number and in this state of tension welcomes any chance of relief however slight. Such a moment comes during Ellen's quarrel with Peter in Act II, Scene i. The music leading up to this has been superimposed on the church service (off) with its in-going voluntary, morning hymn, responses, gloria and benedicite. As the credo is reached, Peter and Ellen start to quarrel; and at this point the rift between the two musical streams widens, the credo being intoned by the Rector and congregation to an F held by the organ, while Ellen cross-examines Peter (in the key of D flat) about the boy's bruises. After a par-

ticularly obstinate clash has developed between the sub-
dominant of Ellen's key and the organ's F, her two-bar
dolce phrase, '*Were we mistaken?*' in which her G flat

Ex. 8

Were we mis-ta-ken when we schemed to solve your life by lone-ly toil?
War's doch nur Täuschung, es ge - läng, durch har-te Ar-beit wärst Du frei?

appears to have modulated to F, has the surprise and relief
of a final reconciliation. This relief is only momentary,
however, for the passage leads directly to Peter's cry of
despair, '*God have mercy upon me!*' (cf. ex. 3) and all the
tumult released by that pregnant musical phrase.

As for the recitative in the opera, Britten's purpose can
best be expressed in his own words:[1] 'Good recitative
should transform the natural intonations and rhythms of
everyday speech into memorable musical phrases (as with
Purcell), but in more stylized music the composer should
not deliberately avoid unnatural stresses if the prosody of
the poem and the emotional situation demand them, nor
be afraid of a high-handed treatment of words, which may
need prolongation far beyond their common speech length,
or a speed of delivery that would be impossible in conversation.' In *Peter Grimes*, there are numerous examples of
both natural and unnatural intonation and rhythm. For
instance, as the orchestra is playing the final bars of Ellen's
air '*Let her among you without fault*', Ellen drops her voice
to a *parlando* level and, turning to the carter, says: '*Mister
Hobson, where's your cart? I'm ready.*' The unforced natural-

---

[1] *Peter Grimes: Sadler's Wells Opera Books, No. 3.*

Ex. 9

ness of this passage should be contrasted with another piece of recitative. At the beginning of Act II, after her short *arioso*, '*Glitter of waves*', she also drops her voice to a *parlando* level and asks Peter's apprentice '*Shall we not go to church this Sunday?*' Her words are set to the glittering toccata-like theme just heard in Interlude III (cf. ex. 2)

Ex. 10

whose wide intervals and syncopated measure are utterly at variance with natural conversational idiom.

The chorus plays an important part in the opera. The opening chorus of Act I, Scene i, sung partly in unison and partly in parallel thirds, is sufficiently stolid with its diatonic hymnlike tune to bring out the drab as well as the picturesque aspect of life in a little fishing port; and the manner in which it is recapitulated at the end of the opera, the whole musical structure being cut through in cross-section at its climax so that it ends with the same abruptness as the East Anglian coast with its eroded cliffs facing the sea, constitutes an essential element in the opera's construction. Later in the opening scene of Act I, at the approach of the storm cone, the chorus is given a simple but moving appeal, '*O tide that waits for no man, spare our coasts!*' But its most impressive moment—and in some ways the climax of the whole opera—comes at the end of the first scene of Act III with its unaccompanied fortissimo shouts of '*Peter Grimes! Peter Grimes! Grimes!*' If this passage is to obtain its full effect, the chorus must be suffi-

ciently strong for its cries to resound through the theatre
and 'lift the roof'. Otherwise, the device of complete
musical silence broken only by Balstrode's spoken words
at the climax of the following scene (Grimes's suicide) loses
some of its power by contrast.

Some critics, after comparing *Peter Grimes* with *Boris
Godunov*, have suggested that *Grimes* is an opera whose
true protagonist is the chorus. But the analogy is mis-
leading. The statement may well be true of Moussorgsky's
opera, for the Russians tend to exalt the collective or com-
munal ideal at the expense of the individual, but not of
Britten's. Although the majority of the inhabitants of the
Borough are prejudiced bigots, they nevertheless remain
closely defined individuals who are absorbed into the
general community only when their finer feelings are sub-
merged by the herd instinct—as on the occasion of the man-
hunt. The changes of focus whereby Balstrode, Boles, the
Rector, Swallow, Keene, Hobson, Mrs. Sedley, Auntie and
her two nieces appear sometimes as individuals (with short
solos to sing), sometimes as neighbours (with parts in an ensemble) and sometimes as members of the general chorus,
are deliberately designed by Slater and Britten as a means
of obtaining characterization in depth.

Whereas in his musical dramas Wagner was thinking
first and foremost of his orchestral texture and his peculiar
form of symphonic development led to an apparently unbroken flow of melody into which the vocal parts had to fit
like additional instruments, Britten's prime concern in
Peter Grimes is to display the voices of protagonists, minor
characters and chorus to the best possible advantage. This
means, not that the vocal writing is necessarily easy and un-
complicated, but that, with the exception of the six Interludes, the orchestra is definitely used in a subordinate position as a means of accompaniment. How important this is
can be seen from the scene in *The Boar* where, thanks to the

preceding Interlude, the orchestra is able to allude to the furious storm outside without drowning the singers or, indeed, making it necessary for them (for the most part) to lift their voices above the level of normal recitative. Despite the use of a full symphony orchestra and of certain symphonic effects in the Interludes, *Peter Grimes* owes its characteristic movement and idiom to Britten's imaginative treatment of the voices.

Peter Grimes himself as portrayed in Slater's libretto is what might be called a maladjusted aggressive psychopath. There is a chasm, which he fails to bridge, between himself and the external world; and Britten has shown much ingenuity in finding appropriate devices to express this maladjustment in musical terms. Peter's disturbed state of mind leads, not only to the fragmentary style of utterance on which his monologue in Act I, Scene ii, and his soliloquy in Act II, Scene ii are built up, but also to a disjunct motion in his vocal line and a tendency to use intervals wider than the octave. The minor ninth seems to be particularly symptomatic of his difficulty in adjusting himself to the outside world, and an upward leap of this interval occurs several times in his narration of the events that led up to

the death of his first apprentice. But when he sees in Ellen a possible solution of his troubles, this interval does not resolve on the octave, but widens to the *major* ninth.

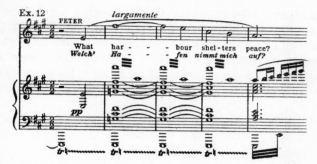

Insofar as Peter is different from the rest of the Borough,
augmentation and inversion are particularly associated

with his music—augmentation when during the inquest in the Prologue he takes the oath and, later, when he joins the round in *The Boar* (Act I, Scene i); inversion in the hut scene (II, ii) when to an inversion of Example 3 he turns on his apprentice boy and accuses him of being the cause of all

Ex.14

PETER

p

You sit there watch-ing me.........
Du sitzst da, starrst mich an.........

his troubles. Another example of inversion deserves special mention: In the Prologue, the chorus is accompanied by the wood-wind with a simple staccato chattering figure (Ex: 15 (*a*)), which clearly becomes associated in Peter's mind with the persecution of Borough gossip. It reappears,

Ex.15

a)

staccato

b) PETER *marcato*

Away from ti-dal waves   a - way from storms
Weit-ab von Wetternot,   von Sturmflut fern

inverted, in his soliloquy at the end of Act I, Scene i (Ex: 15 (*b*)).

Occasionally Britten feels justified in using bitonality to emphasize Peter's maladjustment, and then he sometimes tries to reconcile the simultaneous use of hostile keys by enharmonic means. An excellent example occurs at the end of the Prologue, when Peter and Ellen, left alone in the Moot Hall after the inquest, sing an unaccompanied duet. At first, Peter's key is F minor and Ellen's E major; but as the voices intertwine, Peter, thanks to the enharmonic mediation of A flat and G sharp, is won over to Ellen's key, and

the duet ends with both singing in unison. Exactly the same bitonal clash (F minor against E major) is to be found in the violent tremolo passage for full orchestra that punctu-

ates the chorus's shouts at the end of the first scene of Act III.

A similar example of bitonality reconciled by enharmony occurs in the first scene of Act II. There a simple sequence of notes—E flat, F natural, D natural—is harmonized by chords from the organ in the key of C minor and becomes

the sung gloria in the church service (off). The enharmonic equivalent of this theme—D sharp, E sharp, D sharp, C double sharp—then appears in the theatre orchestra, harmonized in the key of B major, and becomes the accompaniment to Ellen's *arioso*, '*Child, you're not too young to know where roots of sorrow are.*'

These enharmonic and bitonal devices which are used to express Grimes's maladjustment, together with the various passages where by cross-fading two musical streams impinge implicitly, if not explicitly, upon the ear, at first cause a kind of auditory dichotomy on the part of the listener. But when this new idiom has become more familiar and acceptable, it is realized that in *Peter Grimes* Britten has certainly widened the boundaries of opera by introducing new and stimulating ideas culled from cinema and radio technique and has shown himself a remarkably subtle delineator in musical terms of complex psychological states of mind.

The originality of the work remains unimpaired, even after one has made allowances for such unconscious or subconscious echoes as the resemblance between the A Lydian of Peter's '*And she will soon forget her schoolhouse ways*' and the D Lydian of Ping's '*Ho una casa nell' Homan*' in *Turandot*, and the unresolved cadence at the end of Act I Scene i repeated faster and faster until it almost becomes a trill just like the curtain to the first act of *Wozzeck*. This East Anglian story comes from an East Anglian heart, and it is never likely to lose the exciting freshness of its original impact.

CHAPTER III

The Rape of Lucretia

I

When *The Rape of Lucretia* was first performed at Glyndebourne, the programme note explained that Ronald Duncan's libretto had been written 'after the play *Le Viol de Lucrèce* by André Obey and based on the works of Livy, Shakespeare, Nathaniel Lee, Thomas Heywood and F. Ponsard'.

The main Latin sources for this story of Roman virtue outraged by Etruscan lust and treachery are Livy and Ovid; but at the end of the Renaissance, Shakespeare made this story so much his own, partly by direct narration in his early poem *The Rape of Lucrece* and partly by references in some of his later plays (notably *Macbeth* and *Cymbeline*), that echoes of his voice are likely to be heard in any subsequent attempt to dramatize it. This is particularly true of *Le Viol de Lucrèce*, which André Obey wrote in 1931 for Jacques Copeau's Compagnie des Quinze. In fact, the play quotes from Shakespeare's poem such passages as the description of Lucrece asleep in her bed, her arraignment of Opportunity after the rape, and the invocation of Philomel ('*Poor bird . . .*') as she contemplates suicide. To comment on the action, Obey decided to have a Chorus of both sexes, but reduced it from plural to singular numbers, the Male and Female Chorus being endowed with special insight into the characters of Tarquin and Lucrece respectively. In this way, he was able to expand the Shakespearean device of the soliloquy and throw a revelatory beam on the subconscious workings of the two protagonists' minds. At the same time, both Choruses were free to comment on the action; and this they did from a more or less contemporary angle, occasionally quoting fragments of Shakespeare or Livy when it suited their purpose.

Obey arranged his tragedy in four acts, according to the following scheme: *Act I, Scene i.* During the siege of Ardea, two sentinels overhear the Etruscan and Roman generals carousing in a tent and describing how, in the course of a surprise visit to Rome the previous night to make trial of their wives, only the virtue and chastity of Collatinus's wife Lucrece had been triumphantly vindicated. Inflamed by this account, Tarquin steals from the tent and sets off for Rome on his steed. *Scene ii.* The same evening, Lucrece is discovered, spinning, with her maids at home. Tarquin arrives unexpectedly and is offered hospitality for the night. *Act II.* Lucrece's bedchamber: the same night. Tarquin enters her room, wakes and ravishes her. *Act III.* The same scene: the following morning. Lucrece awakens and sends for Collatinus. *Act IV, Scene i.* A commentary, mainly by the Male and Female Chorus, on the revolutionary state of feeling in Rome. *Scene ii.* The same scene as Act I, Scene ii. After telling the story of her rape, Lucrece stabs herself. Brutus, on behalf of the other Romans there present, swears revenge on the Etruscans.

The presence of the Male and Female Chorus on the stage and their commentary on the action made it necessary for the actors to develop a style that could merge almost imperceptibly from acting into mime as occasion demanded and produced a kind of extra dimension that seemed to transcend the normal limitations of realistic stagecraft. As produced by Michel St. Denis for Copeau's company in the early years of the 1930's, *Le Viol de Lucrèce* lives in the memories of those who saw it as one of the masterpieces of twentieth century theatre.

For his libretto, Duncan kept fairly closely to Obey's play. He slightly reduced the number of *dramatis personæ* by doing away with a few of the servants and a pair of sentinels, but adopted without change the device of the Male and Female Chorus. He compressed the action into two acts, instead of four. *Act I; Prologue*. Male and Female Chorus: general exposition. *Scene i*. The generals' tent in the camp outside Rome. (This loosely follows Obey's Act I, Scene i.) *Interlude*. Male Chorus: description of Tarquinius's ride to Rome. *Scene ii*. A room in Lucretia's house in Rome the same evening. (This closely follows Obey's Act I, Scene ii.) *Act II; Prologue*. Male and Female Chorus: further exposition. *Scene i*. Lucretia's bedroom. (This follows Obey's Act II.) *Interlude*. Male and Female Chorus: chorale. *Scene ii*. A room in Lucretia's house the next morning. (This partly amalgamates Obey's Act III and Act IV, Scene ii.) *Epilogue*. Male and Female Chorus: final commentary.

It will be seen that, according to Duncan's scheme, the rape comes three-quarters instead of half way through the action: with the result that, whereas in *Le Viol* there was a long gradual diminution of tension during the last half of the play—especially in Act III where Lucrece soliloquizes alone for a considerable part of the scene—in *The Rape* dramatic interest is built up comparatively slowly during the first act and the action gathers impetus during the second act.

In an essay describing his method of writing the libretto,[1] Duncan maintains that 'the legend of Lucretia has much in common with Etruscan mythology'. He adds: 'Just as fertility or life is devoured by death, so is spirit defiled by Fate. Lucretia is, to my mind, the symbol of the former, Tarquinius the embodiment of the latter.' In a further attempt to magnify the symbolic significance of this simple tale and to universalize its values, he has placed the

---

[1] *The Rape of Lucretia* (commemorative volume) ed. Eric Crozier.

Male and Female Chorus outside the temporal framework of the action and allowed them to submit it to Christian interpretation.

> *Whilst we as two observers stand between*
> *This present audience and that scene;*
> *We'll view these human passions and these years*
> *Through eyes which once have wept with Christ's own tears.*

And from this lofty religious viewpoint, they offer (in the Epilogue) the consolation of general absolution.

FEMALE CHORUS : *Is this all? Is this it all?*

MALE CHORUS : *It is not all.*

> *. . . yet now*
> *He bears our sin and does not fall*
> *And He, carrying all,*
> *turns round*
> *Stoned with our doubt and then forgives*
> *us all.*

The severely dogmatic tone of Duncan's Chorus is far removed from the objective pagan spirit of Shakespeare and Obey; but in the Epilogue it certainly provides the composer with a cue for a musical coda of magnificent solemnity.

Fortified by his experience in writing *Peter Grimes*, Britten laid great store by the close collaboration of poet and composer and in his preface to the published libretto maintained that this seemed to be 'one of the secrets of writing a good opera. In the general discussion on the shape of the work—the plot, the division into recitatives, arias, ensembles and so on—the musician will have many ideas that may stimulate and influence the poet. Similarly when the libretto is written and the composer is working on the music, possible alterations may be suggested by the flow of the music, and the libretto altered accordingly. In rehearsals, as the work becomes realized aurally and visually, other changes are often seen to be necessary'. Duncan's libretto reveals nearly as many variations in its various texts as Slater's libretto for *Peter Grimes*. The initial text is to be found in the libretto published by Messrs. Boosey & Hawkes in 1946, a corrected version of which was printed the same year in the vocal score. The following year, a revised edition of both score and text was issued by Boosey & Hawkes, together with a German translation by Elisabeth Mayer. This is substantially the same text as was reprinted in the commemorative volume of 1948[1] and the library edition of 1953.[2]

The effect of some of these changes has been to make the information imparted by the Male and Female Chorus rather less didactic in tone. For instance, in the first version of the Prologue to Act II, the Female Chorus, reading from a book, explains that:

> *The prosperity of the Etruscans was due*
> *To the richness of their native soil,*
> *the virility of their men,*
> *and the fertility of their women—*
> *See Virgil, Book Eleven, verse five three three,*
> *'Sic fortis Etruria creuit' etcetera.*
> *All authorities agree*
> *that the Etruscan conquest of Rome*
> *dates from six hundred B.C.—*
> *that is, approximately.*

In the revised edition, the last six lines are omitted entirely. Other changes are probably due to the need for simplification. Duncan learned that in his role as librettist he must avoid writing complicated sentences. As he says: 'The poet must drive his metaphor to the point of clarity and contain

---

[1] Published by the Bodley Head.

[2] Published by Faber & Faber.

in one image the condensation of a mood. He must never forget that the audience is listening to both words and music, and that their concentration, thus divided, cannot be imposed on.' An example of such simplification is to be found at the beginning of Act I, Scene i, where the Male Chorus's original comment on the generals' drinking bout—

> The grape's as wanton as the golden boy
> Whom the Naiads drew to the whispers of the well
> But these generals drink to drown his wanton echo.

is later changed to—

> The night is weeping with its tears of stars
> But these men laugh—for what is sad is folly.
> And so they drink to drown their melancholy.

Here, a rather intricate, if not confused, simile has given way to a clearer and simpler contrast between the natural sorrow of the unclouded night and the forced laughter of the generals flushed with wine.

But the main alterations affect two of the characters: Junius and Lucia. In the revised version, Junius's devouring jealousy of Collatinus is established more firmly in Act I, Scene i, and this helps to render more credible his sudden irruption with Collatinus just before Lucretia's suicide in the last scene. Meanwhile, Lucia who appeared in the earlier version as a young, frivolous and slightly over-sexed maid-servant, regains a measure of her not yet lost innocence and is given a charming *arioso*, '*I often wonder whether Lucretia's love is the flower of her beauty*'—her only one in the opera—which helps to establish her character musically.

II

As has already been shown, both natural predilection and economic necessity influenced Britten in deciding to choose an instrumental contingent of chamber orchestra dimensions for *The Rape of Lucretia*. A quarter of a century previously, when Strawinsky, partly for reasons of war-time economy, had felt a similar urge in planning *The Soldier's Tale*, he had chosen representative outer-range instruments from each of the main orchestral groups and had found that seven was his irreducible minimum. *The Soldier's Tale* was accordingly written for violin and double-bass, clarinet and bassoon, cornet and trombone, and percussion. Britten's solution was different: a string quintet, a woodwind quartet (with the flute doubling pic-colo and bass-flute, the oboe doubling cor anglais, and the clarinet bass-clarinet) and a miscellaneous trio consisting of horn, harp and percussion—a dozen players in all—with the *recitativo secco* accompanied by the conductor on a piano. (A similar ensemble was chosen by Menotti about the same time for his operas, *The Telephone* and *The Medium*.)

Although this meant that *The Rape* would be a chamber opera in the sense that every executant (vocalist or instru-mentalist) would be a solo performer, it did not necessarily presuppose intimate chamber conditions of performance. The doublings in the instrumentation of works for sym-phony orchestra increase the volume of sound to only a limited extent—as Strawinsky says in the sixth lecture in his *Poetics of Music*, they thicken without strengthening, and above a certain point the impression of intensity is diminished rather than increased and sensation is blunted. Their main purpose is to blend and bind instrumental tone colour; and this may be compared with the custom of covering oil paintings with a heavy layer of varnish. Just as modern taste is in favour of removing these varnishes to reveal the original colours of a painting in all their unsub-dued vigour, so one would like to think that modern audiences, suffering a revulsion from the inflated performances of super-orchestras, were prepared to demand a scaling-down of forces and to accept the convention whereby instrumental tone colours are presented directly in their primary state without any attempt to blend them before they reach the ear.

In the light of the experience gained in touring *The Rape* in England and abroad, it appeared (according to Eric Crozier) that 'the quality and vitality of the voices with instruments were much better in large theatres than in small. There were no complaints of thinness or raggedness in texture'.[1] On the other hand, there were moments when the voices, instead of being sustained by the blended accompaniment that comes from a full body of strings, had to fight for audibility on equal terms with each solo instrument and were in danger of being drowned or rendered insignificant by the unsubdued tone colour of a handful of instruments. As Edward Sackville-West wrote in the Preamble to *The Rescue*, 'it is, paradoxically, impossible to produce an overall orchestral pianissimo without using a considerable body of instruments, whereas a double *forte* requires only the minimum'.

In short, chamber opera demands the highest virtuoso standards from each individual executant—the slightest lapse is liable to prejudice the total effect. It makes similar demands of its audience too. The equipoise between voices and instruments is too precarious for the listener ever to be lulled into a sense of complete relaxation and security; and many listeners—particularly those reared on a rich diet of lush orchestral fare—are apt to resent the necessity of making this special effort. This is one of the problems that Britten and his collaborators have had to face when producing *The Rape of Lucretia*, *Albert Herring* and *The Beggar's Opera*, and one that they have surmounted with extraordinary success.

---

[1] In *The Rape of Lucretia* (*commemorative volume*) ed. Eric Crozier.

III

Whether the conflict in *The Rape of Lucretia* is spirit
defiled by fate or, more prosaically, Lucretia ravished by
Tarquinius, Britten needed two simply contrasted musical
ideas to express it. He found them by taking the melodic
contents of the interval of the diminished fourth and ar-
ranging the notes in two different ways. The first (*a*), a
descending scale-passage, is identified with Tarquinius; the
second (*b*), a sequence of two thirds in contrary motion,
is the kernel of the Lucretia motif. By extension, the idea

of a scale-passage (whether descending or ascending) becomes identified with the male element, and the idea of
thirds with the female element. This is aptly summarized
in the Prologue, where the Male and Female Chorus sing a

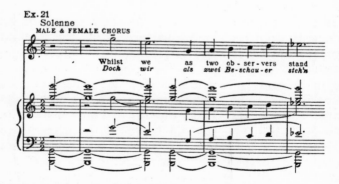

solemn hymn, which combines both elements.

With this key, it is possible to unlock many of the secrets
of the score.

Ex. 22

Lucretia's motif, moving both forwards and backwards, serves as the generals' flamboyant toast in Act I, Scene i (Ex. 22). In diminution, it is frequently used as an accom-

Ex. 23

I

panying figure—for example, in Junius's outburst '*Lucre-tia! I'm sick of that name!*', also in the following comment by the Male Chorus,

> *Oh, it is plain*
> *That nothing pleases*
> *Your friends so much*
> *As your dishonour*

and in the Male Chorus's subsequent apostrophe, when he perceives what is going on in the privacy of Junius's heart and how like an empty vessel it is suddenly flooded with jealousy (Ex.23). Here in the swirling accompaniment, the minor third interval becomes widened progressively to major third, fourth and even fifth. During the same scene, Tarquinius's motif is not much in evidence, though it is clearly referred to in the Male Chorus's opening air which depicts the sultry atmosphere of the evening outside Rome, and three notes of it, repeated by the harp in diminution,

become identified with the noise of the crickets. In the Interlude, however, the male element dominates the furious

ride of Tarquinius and his steed. It is only when horse and rider, after being momentarily checked in their course by the sudden obstacle of the Tiber, plunge into the river and swim across that the Lucretia motif returns, the music of Example 23, now accompanied by the cool metallic hiss of a cymbal tremolo, being repeated to the following words with their prophetic symbolism:

> *Now stallion and rider*
> *Wake the sleep of water*
> *Disturbing its cool dream*
> *With hot flank and shoulder.*

In the second scene, with Lucretia sewing, Bianca and Lucia spinning, and the Chorus interpolating her commentary, inter-linked feminine thirds run riot in the harp

Ex. 26
Molto moderato
LUCRETIA *pp*
Col - la - ti - nus!   Col - la - ti - nus!
pp

accompaniment to the vocal quartet. The rising intonation of Lucretia's apostrophe to her absent husband may be thought of as an altered inversion of the Tarquinius motif,

Ex. 27
MALE CHORUS
pp
His un - ru-ly eyes..... run to her breast   And there with more thirst than manners rest.
Und sein frecher Blick streift ih-re Brust,   *und ruht dort mit un - ver-kohl-ner Lust.*
ppp

which naturally plays an important part a little later when Tarquinius arrives unexpectedly. A particularly subtle touch is to be found in the passage where this motif, preluded by its inversion, is accompanied by a figure made up of both the Tarquinius and Lucretia motifs in diminution (Ex.27). The final series of goodnights, when Lucretia leads Tarquinius to his bedchamber, contains the Tarquinius motif augmented and harmonized with thirds over a ground bass of compound thirds rising by thirds.

At the beginning of the second Act, the interval of the third—and also its inversion, the sixth—are predominant in Tarquinius's air, 'Within this frail crucible of light', sung while Lucretia is still asleep; but when she awakens and in her agitation asks what he wants from her, the music gives an explicit answer, the brassed horn frenziedly attempting

to fill the open interval of the cor anglais's minor third. The new figure formed thereby (*c*) becomes closely identified with Tarquinius's lust during the remainder of the scene, until near its climax Lucretia interrupts him with a broad and dignified rebuke based on the original Tarquinius motif in augmentation (Ex. 30). In the unaccompanied

Ex. 30

quartet with which the scene ends ('*See how the rampant centaur mounts the sky*') will be found a recapitulation of the jealousy theme (Ex. 23) sung by Lucretia, together with fragments of the Lucretia, Tarquinius and lust motifs.

For the opening of the last scene, where Bianca and Lucia greet the sunny morning and then start to arrange the flowers the gardener has brought, both accompaniment and voices describe festoons of rising and falling thirds. When Lucretia enters and is told by Bianca that they have left the orchids for her to arrange, she bursts out hysteric-

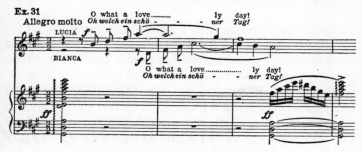

Ex. 31

Ex.32 Vivace

ally, and the music at once refers to the lust theme. Just before her suicide there are two passages where use of the Lucretia motif deserves special notice. The first comes when she asks Bianca if she remembers teaching her as a child to weave garlands of wild flowers. '*Do you remember?*' In a brief aria, Bianca replies; and nothing could sound gayer than this care-free scherzo, with its sparkling accom-

Ex.33 Allegro molto

paniment based on the Lucretia motif in diminution and in a major mode. Later when Collatinus arrives and Lucretia dressed in mourning makes her confession, the Lucretia motif returns to the minor mode, but is tenderly harmon-ized with a major chord (Ex.34). Meanwhile, her silent entry has been made all the more pitiful by the way in which both the regularly moving ground-bass and the hesi-tant sobbing phrases of the cor anglais are formed out of

scale passages (Ex. 35). As she stabs herself, her last words fall in thirds through the compass of two octaves:

> *Now I'll be forever chaste*
> *With only death to ravish me.*
> *See, how my wanton blood*
> *Washes my shame away!*

A funeral march in passacaglia form follows, with a ground-bass that brings to mind the Chorus's solemn hymn (Ex. 21) that has been heard in both Prologues. Over this ostinato, a magnificent sextet is built up, in which each

vocal part is developed with full regard for the characters of the various persons concerned. At the end, special prom-

inence is given to the repeated demi-semiquaver figure;
and this figure persists throughout the Epilogue so that
when the opera ends with a recapitulation of Ex. 21, the
accompaniment is powdered with major and minor thirds
—the minor predominating—spread over the entire orchestral compass, like stars that come out in the firmament
after sunset.

Although these musical germs or cells have been spoken
of as motifs, and their permutations and transformations
traced in some detail, it must not be thought that in *The
Rape* Britten has adopted a comprehensive *leitmotif* system
of construction. Many beauties lie outside the passages
quoted above—to take a single example, the marvellous
lullaby at the beginning of the second Act, one of his most
original and memorable passages. But just as in the *Symphony of Psalms*, Strawinsky used the device of two inter-
linked ascending thirds (rather similar to the Lucretia
motif) to unify the thematic material in each of its three
movements, so Britten has used his motifs to emphasize the
persistence of the fundamental conflict in his theme and to
achieve a remarkably homogeneous texture in his score.

CHAPTER IV

Albert Herring

Albert Herring was intended to be both a companion piece and a contrast to *The Rape of Lucretia*: a companion piece since it is written for the same vocal and instrumental contingent; a contrast in the sense that its subject is comic as opposed to the tragedy of *The Rape*.

Eric Crozier has adapted Guy de Maupassant's short story, *Le Rosier de Madame Husson*, with considerable skill. He has transferred the action from Normandy to East Anglia; and although in the process something of the malicious sparkle of the Gallic original may have been lost, what remains is in most essentials faithful to the letter, if not the spirit, of the original.

The main outline of the plot is soon told. Lady Billows, virtuous herself and the self-appointed guardian of virtue in others, is anxious to select a May Queen in Loxford; but, in default of suitable female candidates, she decides on a May King, and her choice falls on young Albert Herring, who works in a greengrocer's shop and has a reputation for unassailable innocence and chastity. During the May Day celebrations, he is fêted and plied with lemonade that has been surreptitiously laced with rum. So fortified, he breaks out and escapes that evening from the stifling atmosphere of his home. When his absence is discovered the following morning, search parties are sent out. At first, it is feared he may have been killed; but just as his death is being lamented, he arrives back, dirty, dishevelled and defiant after a bibulous night-out.

This is the point where opera and short story begin to diverge. According to Crozier, Albert Herring's night-out consisted only of a pub-crawl, in the course of which he was thrown out of *The Dog and Duck* and *The Horse and Groom*.

Although Herring himself refers to it as 'a night that was a nightmare example of drunkenness, and dirt, and worse', it seems mildly innocuous when contrasted with the virtuous Isidore's escapade. 'Isidore was drunk, dead drunk, besotted after a week of dissipation, and not merely drunk, but so filthy that a dustman would have refused to touch him. . . . He smelt of the sewer and the gutter and every haunt of vice.' This would have set too serious a note for the simple honest fun of Crozier's libretto, and he rightly avoided it. Nevertheless, the character of Herring remains slightly embarrassing; and when the curtain falls, one does not feel convinced that the experience gained in the course of this or any other drinking bout would have been sufficient to free him from the shackles of his painful inhibitions. Isidore eventually died of *delirium tremens*; Albert Herring, one suspects, lived down the momentary scandal of his May Day intoxication and became a respected citizen of Loxford.

Crozier aimed at clarity and simplicity in his libretto and wrote 'to be sung, not to be read from a printed page'. In his series of lectures on *The Poetic Image*, Cecil Day Lewis, speaking from the poet's point of view, has explained the distinction as follows: 'The writing of words for music demands an entirely different technique from the writing of lyric poetry as we now understand the term. Words for music are like water-weed: they only live in the streams and eddies of melody. When we take them out of their element, they lose their colour, their grace, their vital fluency: on paper thay look delicate perhaps, but flat and unenterprising.' It is to Crozier's credit that he understood this, and consequently his libretto is most successful when it is most self-effacing.

Writing in 1938 of Britten's early works, Henry Boys gave it as his opinion that if Britten chose, 'he could undoubtedly become the most original and probably the most successful maker of light music in England since Sullivan'.[1] In *Albert Herring* this prophesy is fulfilled. The music is light and loose, mercurial and full of fun. It recaptures something of the boyish high spirits of his earlier works. '*Avanti!*' cries the composer to his woodwind in the Interlude between the two scenes of Act I, just as eleven years before he had written the same direction in the first movement ('*Rats away!*') of *Our Hunting Fathers*. Sid, the butcher's assistant, laces Albert Herring's glass of lemonade with rum; and a sinister coil of chromatics arises from the orchestra to remind one of the love potion motif in *Tristan und Isolde*. Police Superintendent Budd complains in the last act, when the hunt for Albert Herring is on:

> *Give me a robbery with force*
> *Or a criminal case of rape,*
> *But God preserve me from these disappearing cases!*

And as he mentions rape, the orchestra refers slyly (but *fortissimo*) to the Lucretia motif (cf. Ex. 20 (*b*)).

One of the score's most distinctive characteristics is to be seen in the handling of the recitative. Not only are there examples of every shade of *recitativo secco* and *recitativo stromentato*, but many of these show an extraordinary freedom in rhythm, the voices (*ad libitum*) often going a completely different way from the accompaniment—as in the *recitativo quasi ballata* of Act I, Scene i—while others combine in contrapuntal patterns to form recitative ensembles of great complexity. There are three such ensembles in Act II, Scene i, where each character is directed to sing his or her line at the natural speed of the diction without paying any regard to the other voices or the accompaniment; and the last one, which occurs as the coronation

---

[1]'The Younger English Composers: V. Benjamin Britten', by Henry Boys. *Monthly Musical Record*, October 1938.

feast begins and just before the curtain falls, contains six independent recitative solos, two recitative duets (between Nancy and Sid, and the Mayor and the Police Superintendent), and a canon for the three village children.

In a three-act comic opera like *Albert Herring*, where the music is continuous, the composer has an enormous canvas to fill. As Erwin Stein says, in comic opera 'there are fewer opportunities for slow movements and lyrical expansion than in musical drama'.[1] Although by the use of recitative the composer is able to get over much of the ground at a spanking pace, it becomes all the more necessary for him to strengthen the tension and specific gravity of his music at the nodal points. This is done mainly by increasing the contrapuntal interest of the musical texture. For instance, there are the fugal choruses, '*We've made our own investigations*' and '*May King! May King!*' in Act I, Scene i; in the following scene, the 'pleasures of love' duet, where Nancy and Sid singing in unison are accompanied by a perky woodwind canon at the octave; the fugal Interlude between Scenes i and ii of Act II; and, in particular, the magnificent nine-part threnody in the last Act. This is built up on a ground

Ex. 37

---

[1]'Form in Opera: *Albert Herring* Examined' by Erwin Stein. *Tempo*, Autumn, 1947.

chorus in the minor mode. Above this the individual verses of lament are freely developed. The Vicar's contribution is marked *espressivo*, Nancy's *piangendo*, the Mayor's *marcato ed eroico*, Lady Billows's *brillante*, her housekeeper's *con forza*, the Superintendent's *pesante*, the schoolmistress's *lamentoso*, Sid's *con gravità* and Mrs. Herring's *appassionato*. Towards the end, all these nine characteristic laments, after alteration to fit the major mode, are repeated together over a roll from the *timpani* and fused into a wonderfully intricate knot of polyphony.

It is the opera's special glory that frequently a character or episode is treated with a mixture of satire and sentiment that produces as unforgettable a vignette as a drawing by Rowlandson or a poem by Betjeman. There is the bland and hesitant Vicar trying to reassure Lady Billows on the subject of virtue:

the twittering Miss Wordsworth nervously rehearsing the school children in the festive song:

Ex.39

Mrs. Herring clutching the faded framed photo of her son as a little boy:

Ex. 40

and Albert himself when, returning in the evening from the feast, he enters the greengrocer's shop in the dark and looks round for matches to light the gas to the accompaniment of the exquisite nocturne for bass flute and bass clarinet first heard in the previous interlude:

Ex. 41

It might be thought that in the United States *Albert Herring* would be handicapped by the slang element in its libretto. However that may be, in translation the opera has proved a great success in Germany, and in the original nowhere has it been more enthusiastically acclaimed than in Aldeburgh, which is only a few miles as the crow flies from Loxford itself.

CHAPTER V

The Beggar's Opera

Planned by John Gay as a Newgate comedy, *The Beggar's Opera* was an immediate hit when produced at the Theatre in Lincoln's Inn Fields on January 29, 1728. Its record run of 62 performances, of which the first 32 were consecutive, remained unbroken until the production of *The Duenna* at Covent Garden in 1775. It made the fortunes of a number of persons connected with it. Lavinia Fenton, the original Polly, became the toast of the town and ultimately married the Duke of Bolton. It is calculated that from his four benefit nights (third, sixth, ninth and fifteenth performances), John Gay, the author, received between £700 and £800. Details of the emoluments of Dr. Pepusch, who adapted the music, are not known; but Rich, the manager, seems to have netted a profit of over £6,000 on the first season, and £1,000 or more the following (1728–9) season.[1] This must have contributed substantially to the capital needed a few years later when he promoted the building of the new Covent Garden Theatre.

The fame of *The Beggar's Opera* spread quickly through the provinces and there were performances in Dublin, Glasgow and Haddington in 1728. It was the second piece to be produced at Covent Garden (December 16, 1732). The following year a company took it to the West Indies, where Polly had already gone in Gay's published but for many years unacted sequel, and subsequently it was played in North America. It set a fashion for ballad opera which swept London and persisted for about ten years—at least 120 ballad operas were produced during the period 1728–38

---

[1] These figures are based on the calculations in Sir St. Vincent Troubridge's article 'Making Gay Rich, and Rich Gay', *Theatre Notebook*, October 1951.

—and later the type developed into *pasticcio* opera which flourished during the latter part of the eighteenth century. In both ballad and *pasticcio* operas the predominating role was the playwright's, while the composer had the function of a musical director, who arranged and scored the music selected. But whereas the majority of the tunes used in the ballad operas were popular and anonymous—for instance, fifty-one out of the sixty-nine in *The Beggar's Opera*—the numbers in the *pasticcio* operas had nearly all been composed by contemporary musicians, many of them probably by the arranger himself.

It is not known for certain whether Dr. Pepusch was solely responsible for the music in *The Beggar's Opera* or whether Gay himself played some part in the choice of tunes. The music as published with the libretto consisted of Dr. Pepusch's Overture printed in four-part score and the tunes of the sixty-nine airs given without any indication of harmony. When the songs were separately engraved as Dr. Pepusch's composition, an unfigured bass was added. Other musical editors soon started to make additions and alterations to Dr. Pepusch's score. Dr. T. A. Arne was one of the first; and his dance of prisoners in chains (Act III, Scene xii), for which Dr. Pepusch had specified no music, was later incorporated into the Frederick Austin version. Many others followed.

In default of an authoritative version of the original score, each revival has had to solve afresh the problem of musical presentation. After the first world war, Nigel Playfair produced it at the Lyric Theatre, Hammersmith. The text was carefully revised by Arnold Bennett and all offensive matter removed. Frederick Austin, basing his score fairly closely on a previous version by J. L. Hatton, set about two-thirds of the original tunes in a style that was an elegant *pastiche* of the eighteenth century, scoring them for string quintet, flute, oboe and harpsichord with occasional use of the viola d'amore and viola da gamba. He inserted a number of dances and instrumental interludes, mainly of his own composition; and Lovat Fraser designed a gay colourful setting. The production was pretty and had panache. It proved to be exactly suited to the taste of the post-war public and ran for 1,463 performances, being frequently revived later in the 'twenties and during the early 'thirties.

Yet by 1940, when Glyndebourne produced *The Beggar's Opera* on tour and later brought it to the Haymarket Theatre, London, the Austin version was becoming outmoded. John Gielgud, who on this occasion was the producer, moved away from the emasculated prettiness of the Playfair-Fraser entertainment towards a more realistic treatment of the miseries of London; but he chose the early Victorian period depicted in the style of Cruikshank, and in this inappropriate setting the Austin score was a complete misfit. About the same time Edward J. Dent made a new version of the score at the request of Sadler's Wells; and this was based as far as possible on the original edition. In the event, the Dent version was performed for the first time, not by the Sadler's Wells Opera Company, but by the Clarion Singers, Birmingham, and there have been several subsequent amateur productions.

When Britten decided to make a new adaptation of *The Beggar's Opera* for the English Opera Group in 1948, he turned to Tyrone Guthrie as his collaborator. Guthrie wished to restore the opera's original pungency. He saw it literally as a *beggar's*, if not a *beggars'*, opera—in his own words, 'the expression of people made reckless, even desperate by poverty, but in whose despair there is none the less a vitality and gaiety that the art of elegant and fashionable people often misses'—and he edited the text and planned his production accordingly. The same intention underlay *Die Dreigroschenoper* which Brecht wrote in 1928 for production at the Theater am Schiffbauerdamm, Berlin: but whereas Brecht retained the essential framework of the characters and the plot (although he transferred the period from the early eighteenth century to the last years of Queen Victoria's reign during the Boer War), Kurt Weill removed all the original airs from his score, except the *Morgenchoral des Peachum*, which was based on Peachum's opening song '*Through all the Employments of Life*', and even this was dropped after the dress rehearsal.

As far as Britten was concerned, there was no temptation to cut the original airs. Quite the contrary. He himself said: 'The tunes to which John Gay wrote his apt and witty lyrics are among our finest national songs. These seventeenth and eighteenth century airs, known usually as "traditional tunes", seem to me to be the most characteristically *English* of any of our folk-songs. They are often strangely like Handel and Purcell: may, perhaps, have influenced them, or have been influenced by them. They have strong, leaping intervals, sometimes in peculiar modes, and are often strange and severe in mood. While recognizing that the definitive arrangement of them can never be achieved, since each generation sees them from a different aspect, I feel that most previous arrangements have avoided their toughness and strangeness, and have concentrated only on their lyrical prettiness. For my arrangements of the tunes I have gone to a contemporary edition of the original arrangements by Dr. Pepusch. Apart from one or two extensions and repetitions, I have left the tunes exactly as they stood (except for one or two spots where the original seemed confused and inaccurate).'

In actual fact he used sixty-six out of the sixty-nine airs of the original 1728 version, as against the forty-five set by Austin. Twice he combined two of these airs: the first time to create a duet between Lucy (Air XXXI[1]—'*Is then his*

---

[1]The numbering of the airs is that of the original 1728 edition.

Fate decreed, Sir?") and Lockit (Air XXXII—'*You'll think e'er many Days ensue*'); the second to create a trio between Macheath (Air XXXV—'*How happy could I be with either*') and Polly and Lucy (Air XXXVI—'*I'm bubbled—I'm bubbled*'). Britten's solution of the scene in the condemned hold where Macheath tosses off glasses of wine and bumpers of brandy in the hope of working up sufficient courage to face being hanged upon Tyburn tree is a *tour de force*. The original 1728 version specified a sequence of ten different airs, several of them fragmentary. Austin quite frankly shirked the problem by omitting six of the ten airs: Dent tackled it by giving the complete original tunes to the orchestra as far as possible and allowing Macheath to come in with his fragmentary ejaculations as and when they occurred. Britten's solution was to set the final air '*Green Sleeves*' in such a way that its bass could be used as a ground linking the previous airs. Seven times this ground bass is broken at different points to allow the interpolation of fragmentary airs; twice the fragments fit it exactly; and the tenth time it sinks into its proper place as the bass to the concluding '*Green Sleeves*'.

Although, as the Beggar boasts in the Prologue, there is nothing in the opera so unnatural as recitative, occasional passages of melodrama occur where music underlines spoken dialogue and eases some of the transitions from song to speech and speech to song. There is a particularly ambitious passage of this kind in the form of a series of nine cadenzas introducing eight ladies of the town and a harper in the scene of the tavern near Newgate.

A somewhat similar musical introduction of characters was carried out in Britten's Overture, which replaced Dr. Pepusch's. Guthrie's intention was that after the Beggar had spoken his introduction the curtain would rise and the orchestra would play the Overture while the actors were seen getting ready for the performance and setting the scene of Peachum's Lock. Britten accordingly composed an episodic overture introducing tunes connected with the main characters, starting with Lucy Lockit (fugue) and ending with Mr. Peachum's air '*Through all the employments of life*', which is also the opening number of Act I. The effect is attractive so long as the producer can ensure that the end of the Overture and beginning of the Opera are clearly differentiated so that the actors can get the ictus they need for the start of the action proper.

Another change made by Guthrie was the lengthening of Act I to include the first scene (A Tavern near Newgate) of Gay's Act II. The effect of this was to bring the curtain down at the end of Act I on Macheath's arrest and to confine Act II to the Newgate scenes covering Macheath's imprisonment and escape.

Careful attention has been paid by Britten to the keys of the different numbers. No fewer than thirty-six airs have been presented in their original keys. The transpositions of the remaining thirty have been carried out mainly with an eye to emphasizing two important tendencies—of numbers concerned with Macheath and Polly and their love for each other to gravitate round B flat major and its related keys, and of numbers concerned with Newgate to gravitate round E minor and A major and their related keys. The opera's main tonality is F. The Overture opens in F major; Act I starts with Peachum's first air in F minor; Macheath's scene in the condemned hold is in F minor; and the following trio '*Would I might be hanged*' is in F major. This marks the end of the opera proper, the dance in G minor which comes after the reprieve being of the nature of an afterthought, a kind of jig to wind up the proceedings.

Throughout the opera Britten takes special pains to set off the modal characteristics of the airs and not to force them into the straight-jacket of academic major/minor harmonization. An interesting example of his treatment is to be found in the duet between Polly and Lucy '*A curse attends a woman's love*'. The original tune was '*O Bessy Bell*' and the first half of it is given in Gay's original version of *The Beggar's Opera* as follows:

Ex. 42

Austin, being apparently nervous of the 'strong, leaping intervals' in the vocal part, altered the tune and set it as follows:

Ex. 43

Allegretto

POLLY   LUCY

A curse at - tends that wo - man's love, Who al - ways would be plea - sing. The

pert - ness of..... the bill - ing dove Like tick - ling is..... but teas - ing.

Britten's version is not only faithful to the original, but captures the real non-modulatory spirit of the flattened seventh and sets it in proper relief by the oboe phrase with its false relations:

Ex. 44
Lento

A curse at-tends a wo-man's love, Who al - ways would be plea - sing: The pert-ness of... the bill-ing dove Like tick-ling, is.... but teaz - ing.

Quotations illustrating the numerous ingenuities of Britten's settings of these tunes could easily be multiplied—the augmentations and diminutions, the metric subtleties, the daring harmonic progressions that occasionally seem to modulate against the vocal line, the startling stab of bitonality in the chorus '*Let us take the road*', the use of canon and imitation, the free development of counter themes, the cunning instrumentation, and so on. But even more important than any of these is the fact that Britten still knows when mere cleverness is out-of-place and when it behoves him to be absolutely unaffected and simple. For instance, his setting of the duet between Mrs. Peachum and Polly '*O Polly, you might have toy'd and kist*' is most lovely and haunting. It will be found that here too Britten's vocal line differs from the Austin version, the reason being that Britten has literally followed the original tune '*O Jenny, O Jenny, where hast thou been*' as given in the original editions.

The orchestra for this version of *The Beggar's Opera* consists of flute (doubling piccolo), oboe (doubling cor anglais) clarinet, bassoon, horn, percussion, harp, string quartet and double bass. From it Britten obtains a maximum variety of instrumental effects. Examples that stick in the mind are the tremolo flute motif in Polly's air *'The Turtle thus with plaintive crying'*; the lace-like edging provided by the harp to the sturdy cotillon *'Youth's the season made for joys'*; the sensitive flutterings of the flute in Polly's air *'Thus when the swallow seeking prey'*; the savage unison strings with their dotted quaver motif in Lockit's air *'Thus Gamesters united in friendship are found'*; the rumbling of the low timpani bass accompanying the air sung by that deep drinker Mrs. Trapes *'In the days of my youth'*; the sinister liquid gurgling of the clarinet arpeggi as Lucy urges Polly to *'take a chirping glass'*; and the vibration of the tremolo bell chords, the tolling of which punctuates the trio *'Would I might be hanged!'*

Britten's version of *The Beggar's Opera* is not the definitive version—no version will ever be that[1]—but it is to date not only the most brilliant musical version, but also the one in which the operatic nature of the work has been most successfully emphasized. For the first time in its long history, *The Beggar's Opera* needs singers rather than actors to interpret it; and the result is that, whereas none of the earlier versions made any headway abroad, except in the United States and British Commonwealth, *The Beggar's Opera* in Britten's version has been played by many of the opera-houses in Europe,[2] and the work is at long last becoming universally recognized as one of the masterpieces of comic opera.

---

[1]In 1953 another version of the score was made by Sir Arthur Bliss for the film directed by Peter Brook with Sir Laurence Olivier as Captain Macheath.

[2]Details of these productions are given in Appendix B.

CHAPTER VI

The Little Sweep

The Little Sweep is the opera that forms part of the entertainment for young people called *Let's Make an Opera!* Whereas in *Peter Grimes* the apprentice boy was a mute character, here Sam, the sweep-master's eight-year-old apprentice, becomes the hero of the opera, and a fully vocal hero too.

The story of how a number of children living at Iken Hall, Suffolk, in 1810 meet Sam, a new sweep-boy, while he is sweeping one of the chimneys, and succeed in rescuing him from his bullying master, Black Bob, was based by Eric Crozier, not on Lotte Reiniger's silhouette film *The Little Chimney Sweep* (1935), nor Charles Kingsley's *The Water Babies* (though Britten himself was brought up on Kingsley's book as a boy), nor Elia's mannered essay, *The Praise of Chimney-Sweepers* (1822), but on William Blake's song of innocence, *The Chimney Sweeper*:

> *When my mother died I was very young,*
> *And my father sold me while yet my tongue*
> *Could scarcely cry "'weep!'weep!'weep!'weep!'*
> *So your chimneys I sweep, and in soot I sleep.*

Despite its surface gaiety, the atmosphere of this little opera is surcharged with intense pity and indignation for the plight of the hapless sweep-boy sold into servitude because of his parents' poverty. If to readers of Lamb and Kingsley the note of cruelty implicit in this tale seems rather exaggerated, they will find more than sufficient justification for Crozier's attitude if they consult *A People's Conscience*[1] where the case of the climbing boys is presented on the basis of evidence contained in the reports of various Select

---

[1] By Strathearn Gordon and T. G. B. Cocks, Constable, 1952.

Committees of the House of Commons. No wonder that as
Blake wandered through the London streets he heard

> *How the chimney-sweeper's cry*
> *Every black'ning church appals.*

The practice of using young boys to sweep the more difficult and dangerous flues was not really abolished until the
latter part of the nineteenth century; and as late as June
1949, the month and year in which *Let's Make an Opera!*
was first performed, the last of the chimney boys—Mr.
Joseph Lawrence of Windlesham, Surrey—celebrated his
104th birthday.

It is to the credit of Britten and Crozier that, while not
shirking the fundamental problem of this opera, they present it in such a cheerful and sympathetic guise that the
audience is completely beguiled; and this audience, it must
not be forgotten, includes children and young people as
well as adults.

Sam, the little sweep, is eight years old. It is a party of
half a dozen children, three of them living at Iken Hall and
three of them on a visit there, that rescue him from the flue
where he had stuck and eventually deliver him from his
master. As against these seven child actors—all the boys
with unbroken voices—there are six adult parts, two of
which can be doubled. The cast of eleven is accordingly a
mixture of amateurs and professionals; and Britten and
Crozier had the audacious but brilliant idea to increase the
amateur element by implicating the whole of the audience
in the performance. This they did by giving the audience
four songs to sing in the course of the opera: *The Sweep's
Song* by way of overture, *Sammy's Bath* and *The Night
Song* as interludes between scenes i and ii, and scenes ii and
iii, and the *Coaching Song* that forms the finale.

Such an unorthodox plan could be carried out successfully only if the audience were given an opportunity to

rehearse their songs; and this gave Britten and Crozier the cue they needed for the earlier part of the entertainment. Clearly the opera must be shown in rehearsal; and this in fact was how *Let's Make an Opera!* was first presented at Aldeburgh. Later, however, Crozier revised this first part, expanding it into two acts so as to show quite clearly the conception, writing and composition of the opera as well as its stage production. Although these two acts are in the form of a play, they contain a certain amount of incidental music. For instance, the first scene ends with a musical toast in the form of a round on the words '*Let's Make an Opera!*' and later on the local builder who is roped to play the parts of the Sweepmaster's assistant and the gardener takes part in an audition at which he sings '*Early One Morning*'. Earlier, there is a glimpse of the composer at work on the scene where Sam, just after his rescue from the chimney, begs the children '*Please don't send me up again!*' During the second act, the audience is given a chance not only to learn its four songs, but also to see three of the children's ensembles being rehearsed: so by the time the opera proper is reached, the work of preparation has been so thorough that much of the music is greeted with a thrill of recognition.

The orchestra is smaller even than that used for *The Rape of Lucretia*, *Albert Herring* and *The Beggar's Opera* and consists of a solo string quartet, piano (four hands) and percussion (single player).

The music is not continuous. As in *Paul Bunyan*, there is spoken dialogue between the numbers; and there is practically no recitative.

The score is distinguished by the straightforward appeal of the vocal line; but the setting and presentation of the melodies often show a considerable degree of sophistication. The tunes of all four audience songs are so simple that some of them (particularly the Night Song) bid fair to

attain an independent popularity; but in their operatic setting they are distinguished by metrical and harmonic
touches of considerable subtlety. For instance, each verse
of the first audience song is prefaced by the cry 'Sweep!' and
the opening phrase of the catchy tune is:

But Britten sets it in 5-4 time, which gives a fascinating
contrast between the groups of nine hurrying triplet quav-
ers and the more measured tread of the two crotchets and
makes ingenious use of the fact that a large concourse of
people of all ages singing in unison often produces a slightly indeterminate pitch.

The cry 'Sweep!' is harmonized differently on every appearance, with the result that although the tune never
varies, the song in the course of its five verses modulates
from D minor through B flat major, G minor, E flat major
to D minor (ending on a chord of the major). Ex. 47 shows
the transition between verses three and four:

Another example of the magical effects to be obtained
from shifting harmonies while the tune remains constant
is to be found in the Ensemble '*O why do you weep through
the working day?*' At the end of each verse a three-part
phrase sung by the children leads to Sam's repeated, un-
forgettably poignant cry '*How shall I laugh and play?*' The
first and last verses are given in Ex. 48; and it will be seen
how natural and moving is the clash between the F natural
and the F sharp in the final cadence.

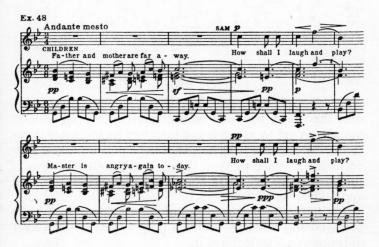

Ex. 48

Although Britten takes considerable pains to protect the
children's voices from anything too complicated in the
way of melody, he does not hesitate to allow them to take
part in a contrapuntal movement like the finale to Scene ii,
which is really a passacaglia on a ground bass formed by
the rising scale of D major (Ex. 49).

Since Purcell produced *Dido and Aeneas* for Josias
Priest's girls' school at Chelsea, no more beautiful opera
for child performers has been written. Its immediate popularity as an entertainment, not only in this country but all

Ex. 49

over the world, has been phenomenal[1]; but what is more difficult as yet to assess is the extent of its influence in introducing children to opera. In some countries a new generation is growing up that, thanks partly to its example, is prepared to accept opera and its conventions as a natural and familiar art form.

The Little Sweep is an opera of innocence—of innocence betrayed and rescued—and it is fully worthy of the singer of innocence who inspired it.

---

[1] See Appendix B.

CHAPTER VII

Billy Budd

I

At the first Aldeburgh Festival in 1948, E. M. Forster gave a lecture on George Crabbe and Peter Grimes. The crowded audience, which included Benjamin Britten, sat on the hard benches of the Baptist Chapel that warm summer afternoon and heard the lecturer talk about the far-reaching alterations Montagu Slater had made when constructing his opera libretto on the basis of Crabbe's poem. Having enumerated some of these changes, he went on to say: 'It amuses me to think what an opera on Peter Grimes would have been like if I had written it. I should certainly have starred the murdered apprentices. I should have introduced their ghosts in the last scene, rising out of the estuary, on either side of the vengeful greybeard, blood and fire would have been thrown in the tenor's face, hell would have opened, and on a mixture of *Don Juan* and the *Freischütz* I should have lowered my final curtain.'[1]

Britten didn't forget these words and when shortly afterwards he contemplated writing another full-scale opera and found his imagination irresistibly kindled by Herman Melville's posthumous novel, *Billy Budd, Foretopman*, it was to Forster as collaborator that he instinctively turned. With characteristic courage this septuagenarian novelist and essayist agreed to set out on a new and hazardous career as opera librettist. Hitherto his experience of dramatic writing had been confined to a couple of open-air pageants; but how deep was his love of music could be seen from the part it played in his novels and essays. (Who, having read *Where Angels Fear to Tread*, could ever forget his account

---

[1]From 'George Crabbe and Peter Grimes' printed in *Two Cheers for Democracy*, Arnold, 1951.

of the performance of *Lucia di Lammermoor* at Monteriano?) The libretto of *Billy Budd* was the joint creation of himself and Eric Crozier; and, as might be expected after his remarks on *Peter Grimes*, it was conscientiously faithful to the spirit and even the letter of the original.

Melville was an old man of sixty-nine when after twenty years' silence as a novelist he began to write his last story. The first draft of the various Billy Budd manuscripts was dated November 16, 1888; the main revision was begun on March 2, 1889; and the story finished on April 19, 1891, a few months before Melville's death. F. Barron Freeman has shown[1] how the initial short story of sixteen sections, *Baby Budd, Sailor*, was expanded into the novel of thirty-one sections generally known as *Billy Budd, Foretopman*.

'An Inside Narrative' Melville called it, going out of his way to suggest that the story he was telling was a true one and that this was the reason for some of its crudities—'The symmetry of form attainable in pure fiction cannot so readily be achieved in a narration essentially having less to do with fable than with fact.' Indeed, it appears almost as if he were bent on a work of rehabilitation, for he quotes a completely distorted account of the events that led to the execution of Budd, purporting to come from a contemporary naval weekly chronicle at the end of the eighteenth century, and explains that so far this had been the only record of this strange affair. But it would appear that the actual events on which *Billy Budd, Foretopman* is based took place, not in the British Navy at the time of the mutinies of Spithead and the Nore which is the period Melville has chosen for the setting of his story, but in the American Navy nearly half a century later; and the intensity of his interest in what came to be known as the Mackenzie Case can be appreciated from the fact that his first cousin, Guert

---

[1] *Melville's Billy Budd*, edited by F. Barron Freeman. Harvard University Press, 1948.

Gansevoort, was one of the lieutenants on board the brig-of-war *Somers* in 1842 at the time of the so-called mutiny.

The Mackenzie Case is specifically referred to in *Billy Budd, Foretopman*. In explaining the difficulty the drum-head court experienced in trying Billy Budd, Melville wrote: 'Not unlikely they were brought to something more or less akin to that harassed frame of mind which in the year 1842 actuated the commander of the U.S. brig-of-war *Somers* to resolve, under the so-called Articles of War, Articles modelled upon the English Mutiny Act, to resolve upon the execution at sea of a midshipman and two petty-officers as mutineers designing the seizure of the brig. Which resolution was carried out though in a time of peace and within not many days sail of home. An act vindicated by a naval court of inquiry subsequently convened ashore. History, and here cited without comment.' Melville's care in explaining the reasons that actuated the captain of the *Indomitable* in giving his evidence and the drumhead court in reaching their verdict seems indirectly to be aimed at vindicating Gansevoort who as the chief aide of Captain Mackenzie against the 'mutineers' on the *Somers* came in for a good measure of subsequent criticism. It is perhaps worth noting that in June 1888, just five months before Melville started to write *Baby Budd, Sailor*, the case was reopened by the publication of an article by Lieutenant H. D. Smith in the American Magazine entitled *The Mutiny on the Somers*. As by then Gansevoort had been dead for twenty years, Melville must have felt that no time was to be lost if he wished to present the events in their proper perspective.

But this material could be used only after it had been digested and assimilated to its fictional purpose. As Free-man says, 'the "inner" drama of Billy Budd uses the Mackenzie Case in the same way that it uses *The Naval History of Great Britain* by William James and Melville's own *White Jacket:* as a factual source on which to build an "interior" drama of the forces of fate'.[1]

Here, as in *Peter Grimes*, the grit of actuality—actual persons and actual incidents—was apparently the prime cause of the long process of artistic secretion that built up, first, an independent literary work and, subsequently, an opera; and it would seem that, consciously or subconsciously as far as Britten was concerned, the actual element behind the fictional treatment still retained a powerful germinating force.

The action in *Billy Budd* takes place on the seventy-four H.M.S. *Indomitable* during the summer of 1797. This was the moment when the mutinies of Spithead and the Nore had just occurred. Conditions in the English Navy were particularly brutalizing, cruel and horrible then, and there is little doubt that the men's grievances were justified; but the authorities were naturally appalled by the hint of revolution at a time when every ounce of energy had to be put into the life-and-death struggle with France.

The *Indomitable* is at sea alone, on her way to join the Mediterranean fleet. Like so many of the ships in the Navy at that time, she is short of her full complement of men : so when a passing merchantman named *Rights-of-Man* is sighted, a boarding party is sent off, and among others Billy Budd is impressed from her crew. Billy is a handsome, pleasant fellow, sound in heart and limb, whose only physical defect is an occasional stammer. He gets on well with everyone on board ship, and everyone likes him—except the master-at-arms, John Claggart. From the outset Claggart pursues him with hidden but implacable malevolence. Natural depravity is bent on corrupting natural innocence and encompassing its downfall. But in plotting Billy's destruction, he reckons without the ship's captain, Edward Fairfax Vere, a bachelor of about 40, known throughout

---

[1] F. Barron Freeman, *op. cit.*

the Navy as 'Starry Vere'. A cultured, aristocratic man, popular with both officers and men, and a shrewd judge of character, Vere immediately sees through Claggart's vamped up charges against Billy. He confronts the sailor with the master-at-arms in his cabin; but the horror of Claggart's false accusation so staggers Billy that it brings out his lurking defect and his power to answer is momentarily taken from him by his stammer. He stands there, tongue-tied, until a kindly gesture from the Captain releases something inside him, and he strikes Claggart a fierce blow with his naked fist. Claggart falls—dead. Captain Vere immediately summons a drumhead court. Billy is tried under the articles of war for striking and killing his superior in grade and is condemned to be hanged from the yardarm, a sentence that is carried out at dawn the following day.

The most important respect in which Forster and Crozier have departed from Melville's story is by letting Vere live to a ripe old age—according to Melville, he was mortally wounded in a sea-fight a few years later, just before Trafalgar—and introducing him in a Prologue and Epilogue where he appears as an old man ruminating on the past. At first he finds it difficult to recall the details of those early days; but what remains indelibly impressed on his mind is that in the faraway summer of 1797 someone had blessed him, someone had saved him. Who was it? As recollection comes crowding back, he remembers his old ship the *Indomitable* and the strange, sad story of Billy Budd.

The device of this Prologue and Epilogue is important for a number of reasons. In the first place, the sea in *Billy Budd* is an isolating medium, the element on which the all-male microcosm, the crew of the *Indomitable*, depends for its temporary suspension. To see the ship from without, alone in the centre of its circumscribing horizon, it is necessary to provide the audience with a view-point outside the field of immediate action. Secondly, the final scene (the hanging) is so tense and its impact so overwhelming that time is needed for the audience to recover. Thirdly, the fact that the action is seen through the eyes of an old man who calls it to mind after the lapse of many years parallels the case of Melville himself composing the story at the age of seventy a short time before his death. Finally, it places the Captain at the centre of the action, showing him caught on the horns of a cruel dilemma. As sole witness of Claggart's death, he finds fate has thrust on him the power of life or death over a human being of whose essential innocence he is fully convinced. The iron discipline of duty prevails over the dictates of his heart—what Melville calls 'the feminine in men'—and he allows Billy to die. The fact that Billy understands and forgives him may be the means of his ultimate salvation, but cannot completely reassure him, for (as he cries out in the Epilogue) he could have saved him, and Billy knew it.

This focussing on Vere puts him into what Henry James called 'the compositional centre'[1] of the drama; and the heroic aspect of the character is accentuated by the vocal casting. Vere is a tenor; Claggart, as befits the villain of the piece, a bass; Billy, a baritone. (In this connection it is interesting to note that in his one-act opera, *Billy Budd* (1949), Ghedini cast Vere as bass, Claggart as tenor and Billy as baritone.)

Some of the overtones in Melville's descriptions of the characters have been dropped. For instance, he more than once implies that the relationship of Vere to Budd is like that of father to son—this is particularly stressed when Vere communicates the finding of the court to the condemned sailor, and Melville suggests that at that moment Vere may have 'caught Billy to his heart even as Abraham may have caught young Isaac on the brink of resolutely

---

[1]Cf. p. 86.

offering him up in obedience to the exacting behest'[1]—but
Forster and Crozier omit this, and in any case such an implied relationship would be contradicted by the vocal casting.

There certainly appear to be sufficient indications of unconscious or latent homosexuality in Melville's description
of Claggart to justify Freeman's statement that 'the psychological key to Claggart's antipathy is not conscious sup-
pression but unconscious repression of a perverted desire
for the boy whose downfall he plotted'[2]; but most of these
indications are missing from the opera libretto, though
Forster and Crozier plumb the depths of Claggart's character in the introspective monologue they given him in Act II,
Scene ii '*O beauty, O handsomeness, goodness!*' No such
soliloquy occurs in Melville; but there is excellent operatic
precedent for it in Iago's Credo in Verdi's *Otello*. Claggart
sings, '*If love still lives and grows strong where I cannot enter
what hope is there in my own dark world for me?*' So beauty,
handsomeness, goodness, as personified by the Handsome
Sailor, must be destroyed. In the libretto the clash between
the two men is shown to be one facet of the eternal struggle
between the powers of good and evil. As W. H. Auden
wrote in his poem *Herman Melville:*[3]

> *Evil is unspectacular and always human,*
> *And shares our bed and eats at our own table,*
> *And we are introduced to Goodness every day,*
> *Even in drawing-rooms among a crowd of faults;*
> *He has a name like Billy and is almost perfect*
> *But wears a stammer like a decoration:*
> *And every time they meet the same thing has to happen;*
> *It is the Evil that is helpless like a lover*
> *And has to pick a quarrel and succeeds,*
> *And both are openly destroyed before our eyes.*

---

[1] It is worth remembering that the first work Britten composed after
Billy Budd was Canticle II: Abraham and Isaac.
[2] F. Barron, Freeman *op. cit.*
[3] From *Another Time*.

One further change made by Forster and Crozier should here be noted. It was necessary for them to include in their libretto both the novice who receives a flogging for dereliction of duty (a passage in *Billy Budd, Foretopman* that is much more reserved and moderate in tone than the comparable passage in *White Jacket* describing the scourging of young Peter of the mizzentop) and the afterguardsman who comes to Billy at night to bribe him to join the mutineers. But whereas in Melville these two characters, though rather shadowy, are quite distinct, in the libretto they are fused together. Humiliated and cowed by his experience, the novice is driven by the fear of further punishment to agree to become Claggart's cat's paw and by tempting Billy to compromise and betray him. A minor character admittedly, but one that Forster and Crozier portray 'in the round'.

The *Billy Budd* libretto is written almost entirely in prose. The only exceptions are the words of some of the interpolated shanties, a few free verse passages, Claggart's blank verse denunciation of Billy to the Captain, and the Ballad of Billy in the Darbies, twenty lines chosen from the thirty-two-line poem with which Melville's narrative ends. The realistic treatment of a subject at one or two removes from actual fact seems to have imposed a predominantly prosaic idiom on the librettists. Some of Melville's dialogue has been preserved intact: e.g. phrases like *Handsomely done, my lad. And handsome is as handsome did it, too!— Jemmy Legs is down on you!—A man-trap may be under his ruddy-tipped daisies.—Fated boy, what have you done!— Struck by an angel of God! Yet the angel must hang!* And there are even one or two passages where Forster and Crozier have based their text on some of Melville's discarded drafts. For instance, in the gun-deck scene, Billy tells his friend Dansker of the Chaplain's visit. '*Chaplain's been here before you—kind—and good his story, of the good*

boy hung and gone to glory, hung for the likes of me.' This is
a direct citation from one of the discarded fragments of the
Ballad of Billy in the Darbies :

> *Kind of him ay, to enter Lone Bay*
> *And down on his marrow-bones here and pray*
> *For the like of me. And good his story—*
> *Of the good boy hung and gone to glory,*
> *Hung for the likes of me.*

It might have been thought that the predominance of
prose would have tended to make the opera ponderous and
heavy; but this is not so. Those prose sections that are dealt
with on the near-declamation level proceed quickly and
lightly: those that are set as passages of *arioso* or as ensembles take on a lyrical quality. Persons who have not
seen the text printed as prose in the libretto would find it
difficult to believe that such numbers as the post-flogging
trio for the Novice, his friend and a small chorus of sailors
with its refrain '*Lost for ever on the endless sea*' (I, i), or the
duet between the Sailing Master and the First Lieutenant
'*Don't like the French*' (II, i), or the '*We've no choice*' trio
between the First and Second Lieutenants and the Sailing
Master at the end of the court-martial (III, ii), or Billy's
farewell to life (IV, i) are not written to a definite metrical
scheme embellished with rhyme or assonance. The prose is
so supple and lissom in texture that it seems to take on
some of the attributes of verse; and, in fact, as pointed out
above, verse fragments are occasionally to be found em-
bedded in it.

II

There is an analogy, though perhaps it should not be
pushed too far, between the four acts of this opera and the
four movements of a symphony—for instance, Britten's
own *Spring Symphony*. The first act is expository, all the
characters being introduced singly or in groups. The second

act is the equivalent of a slow movement: it is a reflective serenade below decks in two parts, the first scene showing the Captain and some of his officers enjoying an after-dinner conversation, during which they hear distant singing from the berth deck, and the second showing the sailors singing shanties before slinging hammocks and turning in for the night. Part of the third act serves as a scherzo, namely the whole of the chase after the French frigate and the call to action stations. The fourth act provides the climax and *dénouement*.

Each act is a complete and continuous movement. Where an act is divided into two scenes (as in Acts II, III and IV), there are orchestral interludes to ensure musical continuity, but none of these is so extended as the interludes in *Peter Grimes*. To bind the various acts more closely together, the openings of Acts II and IV echo the closing bars of Acts I and III respectively. The only real caesura comes plumb in the middle of the opera—between Acts II and III.

The opposition between what Melville (in a discarded draft) called 'innocence and infamy, spiritual depravity and fair repute' lies at the heart of Britten's score. The opening bar of the Prologue with its quiet rippling movement contains a clash between B flat and B natural which typifies this struggle.

In its context this at first appears to be a bitonal passage in E flat major and C major; but later it is seen that in reality the clash is much sharper and more powerful—B flat major against B minor—and this is confirmed by another passage in the Prologue where a bitonal B flat major/B minor chord

thrice repeated encloses a musical phrase later to be
associated with Claggart, the first part of which is related
to the first of the two keys and the second part (the descending fourths) to the second.

At the beginning of Act I when the lights go up on the *Indomitable* with the men holy-stoning her maindeck, the
same notes are there; but now the B flat has suffered an enharmonic change to A sharp and the chord has lost its bitonal implications.

The bitonal clash between two keys with their roots a
semitone apart is closely associated with Claggart's hatred
for Budd. Before Claggart's first entry (I, i) the orchestra is
playing a theme in G major connected with the boarding
party; but as soon as he is addressed by the First Lieutenant, the music clouds over and the key changes to G sharp
minor. The same key relationship governs the initial airs of
the two characters: Billy's exultant '*Billy Budd, king of the
birds*' opens in E major; Claggart's '*Was I born yesterday?*'
in F minor. Similarly, the A major fight between Billy and
Squeak in the first scene of Act II is interrupted by Claggart's B flat arrival; and a few bars later as the men sling
their hammocks in the bays, a sailor (off) sings s shanty
'*Over the water, over the ocean*' in E major, while the or-

chestra is still meditating in F minor on the way Claggart
has just lashed out at one of the boys with his rattan. In the
following act the temperature of the music drops each time
Claggart approaches the Captain in order to denounce
Budd, and the key drops too—this time from G minor to
F sharp minor, not major.

The enharmonic change from B flat to A sharp that was
noted at the beginning of Act I (see Ex. 52 above) occurs in
reverse at the end of Act IV Scene ii just after Billy has been
hanged at the yardarm. This is one of the most astonishing
and frightening moments in the opera. Melville describes
how at that moment an inarticulate noise like 'the freshet-
wave of a torrent suddenly swelled by pouring showers in
the tropical mountains' burst forth from the men massed on
the ship's open deck. In a wordless fugal stretto sung so
quickly that they sound like a pack of wild beasts, the
sailors seem for the moment to be on the verge of mutiny.
(This passage is in E major.) But the officers order all hands
to pipe down, and the command is given on B flat. For
some bars an attempt is made to assimilate this note en-

Ex. 53

harmonically as an A sharp into the Lydian mode of E: but
ultimately force of habit is too much for the men, they obey
the command and disperse, and the music resignedly modulates to the key of B flat major. At this point the music
pivots on A sharp/B flat as if on the hinge of fate.

The final resolution of this bitonal conflict comes at the
end of the Epilogue. Once again the phrase formerly associated with Claggart is enclosed by the bitonal chord (as in
Ex. 51); but this time Claggart's descending fourths have
disappeared, and in their place there is a fanfare—fanfares
in this score are usually associated with Billy Budd—spread
over the common chord of B major. At the same time
Vere's voice is accompanied by a figure earlier associated
with Billy's song of farewell (IV. i), with the result that the
final cadence contains a double clash—B major against B
flat major, and B flat major against A major—and the ultimate resolution on B flat major comes with all the force
and finality of a double resolution.

Ex. 54

Just as there is an occasional enharmonic ambivalence
about the music, so there is sometimes an ambivalence
between the music and the action, and the music and the
words. A problem posited by the action may receive its
solution in purely musical terms; and the listener must be
prepared to recognize and accept this.

For instance, it is rewarding to examine the musical and psychological metamorphoses of a simple musical phrase of a fifth and a semitone. In the Prologue Vere as an old man is bewildered and troubled as he tries to remember what he did in the far-off case of Billy Budd, and why he did it.

Right at the beginning of Act I the phrase appears in the shanty sung by the sailors holystoning the deck.

When Billy Budd is impressed, he shouts a farewell to his old comrades on the *Rights of Man* and his words fall naturally into the simple tune of the shanty.

Some of the officers on the *Indomitable*, however, misunderstand this spontaneous greeting of Billy's and take it as an unbecoming reference to the liberal and suspect views expressed by Thomas Paine in his book *The Rights of Man;* and as the chorus echoes Billy's phrase, they order the decks to be cleared. Henceforward this innocuous phrase is associated with the idea of mutiny. The officers when discussing a glass of wine with the Captain after dinner, identify it with Spithead and the Nore (II. i).

The oboes bring it back in sinister guise when the Novice tempts Billy to join the gang which he says is plotting mutiny on the ship (Ex. 59 (*a*)); the muted trumpets transmute it into glittering guineas to bribe him (Ex. 59 (*b*)).

When Claggart confronts Billy before Captain Vere and accuses him of mutiny, the motif has become the skeleton of the phrase.

Its final appearance, apart from a repetition of Ex. 55 in the Epilogue, is in the scene already mentioned that takes place immediately after the hanging; and there it forms the subject of the wordless fugal stretto.

Ex. 61

It has already been suggested that fanfares and sennets
are closely associated with Billy Budd himself. The air is
filled with these calls when the boarding party returns from
The Rights of Man bringing Billy as an impressed man.
Simple arpeggio figures usually accompany his songs—
e.g. '*Billy Budd, king of the birds!*'; the passage in his duet
with Dansker (II. ii) where he sings '*Ay! and the wind and
the sails and being aloft and the deck below so small and the
sea so wide*'; his duet with the Captain when he thinks he's
about to be promoted (III. ii); his Ballad in the Darbies,
and his song of farewell (IV. i). All these are obvious
instances, so obvious that it would hardly seem worth
while mentioning them, were it not for the astonishing
transformation of this device at the end of Act III Scene ii.

Billy is in a stateroom at the back of the cabin where the
drumhead court has been held, and it is left to Captain
Vere to communicate the finding of the court to him.
Melville says that 'what took place at this interview was
never known'; and Forster and Crozier follow Melville in
this, leaving the death sentence to be communicated to him
off-stage at the end of the act. Britten could have ignored
the problem and allowed the curtain to fall immediately
after Vere's exit; but he chose to tackle it musically
and keeps the curtain up for over a minute on an empty
stage, while slow heavy chords for the whole orchestra, or
strings, or woodwind, or brass, or horns, ranging through
many degrees of volume, tell of the fatal interview behind
the closed door. As can be seen from the few bars quoted,
the passage is really a widely spread arpeggio of F major,
harmonized with chromatic intensity and so tremendously
augmented as to give the effect of a simple signal seen

through an extremely powerful telescope—a rainbow of hope.

Ex. 62

As for the chords themselves, smaller groups of them appear in the following act to accompany Billy's farewell to the world—'*I'm strong, and I know it, and I'll stay strong, and that's all, and that's enough*'—and also at the end of the Epilogue when Vere sings '*But I've sighted a sail in the storm, the far-shining sail, and I'm content.*'

One further example of ambivalence deserves special mention.

Perhaps the most moving moment in the first act is the compassionate trio after the Novice's flogging between the Novice himself, his friend and a small group of sailors.

Ex. 63

The saxophone melody reappears in the second act when Claggart threatens the Novice with a further flogging if he refuses to tempt Billy. After this scene the Novice never reappears; but when at the end of the third act Vere sings '*Beauty, handsomeness, goodness, it is for me to destroy you.*

*I, Edward Fairfax Vere, captain of the "Indomitable", lost
with all hands on the infinite sea',* the Novice's phrase reappears in a turbulent orchestral interjection and provides

a poignant comment on the brutality of the punishment
devised by man for man.

Any analysis of the score of *Billy Budd,* however pene-
trating, would fail in its purpose if it gave the impression
that the opera is abstruse or difficult to listen to. The scoring is light and transparent throughout. As soon as the
lights go up on Act I, the music captures the feeling of a
ship at sea: the shrill sound of the wind in the rigging, the
bustle of life on deck, and the underlying swell of the
ocean. The second act with its two beautifully interlocked
serenades, shows first the officers and then the men during
the quiet interval between supper and sleep when there is
time to relax and meditate. The third act starts with an
alarum that is none the less exciting for being in vain.
After the exhilaration of the chase after the French frigate,
the mood of frustration induced by waiting returns with
the mist, and in this atmosphere Vere witnesses the drama
of Claggart and Budd unroll before his eyes with the in-
evitability of fate and is powerless to intervene.

The final act is brief—in the vocal score there are only
thirty-nine pages for the two scenes of Act IV and the
Epilogue, as against 309 pages for the rest of the opera—
but everything in it is placed with an unerring sense of
effectiveness. Billy's Ballad in the Darbies is one of Britten's happiest inventions—a slow, sleepy tune to a low-
pitched, sluggish accompaniment that changes its chords

reluctantly as Billy sings '*Roll me over fair. I'm sleepy and the oozy weeds about me twist*'.

Some critics have suggested that it would have been an improvement if Budd, being the hero of the opera, had been cast as a tenor instead of a baritone; but in that case the setting of this Ballad would undoubtedly have suffered, for the low pitch at which it is written and the tone colour of that particular range of a baritone voice are essential to its effect.

The march to which the whole crew assembles at the beginning of Act IV Scene ii to witness the hanging is a fugato mainly for percussion, and its characteristic rhythm containing both triplets and quintuplets spills over into the Epilogue, where its pianissimo roll on the timpani accompanies Vere's recital of Billy's burial at sea and forms the wake of the *Indomitable* as she disappears from view in the minds of the audience.

There is one final comment to be made. When it was known that Britten was writing an opera with an all-male cast, there were some who prophesied failure because they claimed that without women's voices the monotony of tone colour would be unendurable. After the first performance of *Billy Budd* this particular criticism disappeared because in fact it was discovered that Britten's writing for this all-male cast was extraordinarily varied. Apart from the seventeen individual characters, who include five tenors, eight baritones, one bass-baritone and three basses he calls for a main-deck chorus of thirty-six, a quarter-deck chorus of fourteen, four Midshipmen, whose voices should appear to be breaking, and ten powder-monkeys, who are not required to sing, but whose shrill chattering voices form an important element in the build-up of the big chorus in Act III Scene i when chase is given to the French frigate.

The verdict on *Billy Budd* must be that between them Forster and Crozier wrote one of the best and most faithful librettos to be based on a literary masterpiece, and Britten created a score of outstanding psychological subtlety. The work rouses a wide range of emotions; but perhaps the dominant one is compassion—compassion for the weak and unfortunate, for those who are homeless, the victims of fate; compassion for suffering in all its forms.

CHAPTER VIII

Gloriana

I

In the past there have been few English dynastic operas and few occasions on which a reigning monarch has played a direct part in supporting opera in this country.

Albion and Albanius was a dynastic opera in honour of what Dryden called 'the double Restoration of Charles II' (Albion). Unfortunately Charles's death delayed its production until 1865, when Dryden introduced some appropriate references to James II (Albanius) and it was produced at the Queen's Theatre in Dorset Garden; but its run was brought to an untimely conclusion by the news of the rising of the Duke of Monmouth in the west. In any case, the music provided by Louis Grabu seems to have been so indifferent that no one regretted the opera's demise. The same criticism seems to have been true of Clayton's setting of Addison's *Rosamond* (1707): but here the dynasty celebrated was that of Sarah, Duchess of Marlborough.

When the Hanoverians succeeded to the throne, Handel gained a considerable measure of royal favour; and both George I and II contributed towards the cost of Italian opera in London between 1722 and 1744, the royal subscription of £1,000 being paid annually to The Royal Academy of Music (Undertakers of the Opera), except in 1734 when it was paid personally to Handel himself and the three years 1739–41 when it lapsed.[1] Handel's only attempt at a dynastic opera was *Riccardo Primo, Re d'Inghilterra* (1727) written on the occasion of George II's Coronation.

[1]See 'Finance and Patronage in Handel's life' in *Concerning Handel* by William C. Smith. Cassell, 1948.

After Handel's death Royal patronage declined for about a century: but, thanks largely to the musical sensibility of the Prince Consort, Queen Victoria started her reign by displaying an active interest in opera. During her husband's lifetime, she frequently attended performances at Covent Garden and Drury Lane, and in particular gave her patronage to the various Pyne-Harrison seasons of English opera that started in 1857. When Wallace's *Lurline* was successfully produced at Covent Garden in 1860, she is reported to have advised Louisa Pyne and William Harrison to make money out of it as long as it would run. But the Prince Consort's death in 1861 put an end to her public theatre-going; and although there were occasional command performances at Windsor Castle towards the end of the century, her interest in English opera seems to have been confined to urging Sullivan to drop his operetta partnership with Gilbert in order to write a 'grand' opera, a royal command which led to the production of *Ivanhoe* (1891).

Queen Alexandra took a keen personal interest in opera. She frequently attended performances at the Royal Opera House during Edward VII's reign; so it is not altogether surprising to find that *La Fanciulla del West* (1910) was dedicated *A Sua Maestà La Regina Alessandra d'Inghilterra —rispettoso omaggio di Giacomo Puccini*. But at this period so few English operas were performed in London that it is doubtful if members of the Royal Family could have seen any at Covent Garden, even if they had particularly wanted to.

There was accordingly no precedent for the fact that in May 1952 Her Majesty Queen Elizabeth II gave her approval to the suggestion that Britten should write a Coronation opera on the theme of Elizabeth I and Essex, and that later Her Majesty agreed to accept the dedication of the work and to attend its first performance at a special gala on June 8, 1953, in honour of her Coronation.

An English historical subject was something of a novelty so far as English opera was concerned. Different historical periods had often been used as settings for romantic operas but if historical characters and episodes were introduced, they were usually treated with the same freedom as if they were creations of fiction. It is true that during the Commonwealth Sir William Davenant evolved a new type of operatic representation based on comparatively modern historical subjects—*The Siege of Rhodes* (1656), *The Cruelty of the Spaniards in Peru* (1658), and *The History of Sir Francis Drake* (1659)—but his example was not followed up. This lack of initiative was all the more surprising since the Elizabethan playwrights, particularly Shakespeare, had given a strong lead in the writing of English historical plays.

Later on, there was the example of Russian musicians to note. The nationalist school of the nineteenth century frequently chose patriotic themes for its operas, e.g. Cavos's *Ivan Susanin* (1815), Glinka's *A Life for the Czar* (1836), Rimsky-Korsakov's *The Maid of Pskov* (1873), Moussorgsky's *Boris Godunov* (1874), and Borodin's *Prince Igor* (1890). A similar tendency might easily have been observable in nineteenth-century Italy, had not the local Censorship proved so sensitive over the political implications of historical subjects.

The twentieth century has produced new standards of historical accuracy and new methods of historical research. Invention and fancy are at a discount: it is selection that counts—and presentation.

Just as Pushkin based his tragedy of *Boris Godunov* on Nicolai Karamsin's *History of Russia*, so William Plomer went to J. E. Neale and Lytton Strachey for his sources. *Elizabeth and Essex* was in fact the starting-point for the libretto of *Gloriana*. Strachey had tried to outline this epi-

sode of Elizabeth's old age—'a tragic history' he called it—
with something of the detachment and self-sufficiency of a
work of art; but the bewildering richness of life in Elizabethan England seems to have defeated him. He himself
confessed that 'the more clearly we perceive it, the more
remote that singular universe becomes'.[1] The Elizabethans
were more paradoxical, elusive, ambiguous and irrational
than the Victorians; and profound social changes in the
intervening period had left him little or nothing to debunk.
Elizabeth and Essex is not a completely successful book;
but it contains numerous dramatic cues, and it was this
aspect of it that appealed so strongly to Britten and Plomer.

In the process of selection, a number of important persons and episodes had to be discarded. Of these, perhaps
the most notable was Sir Francis Bacon. His character was
too subtle, complex and compelling, and would have demanded too much attention in the opera. But it must be
admitted that his total disappearance—and there is no
mention of him in the libretto—seriously weakens Essex's
character. For a considerable time he loomed like a grey
eminence in the background, and many of Essex's squabbles
with the Queen seem to have been concerned with her un-
willingness to listen to his pleas that Bacon should be
granted preferment. Yet when the final crisis came and
Essex was arraigned for high treason, Bacon acted without
scruple or hesitation as counsel for the prosecution, and by
his handling of the case helped to bring his former bene-
factor to the block on Tower Hill.

A less important person who was omitted was Elizabeth's godson Sir John Harington. In *Portraits in Miniature*, Strachey described one of Sir John's adventures as
follows:

'He was summoned by Essex to join his ill-fated expedition to Ireland, in command of a troop of horse. In

---

[1] Lytton Strachey, *Elizabeth and Essex*.

Ireland, with a stretch of authority which was bitterly resented by the Queen, Harington was knighted by the rash Lord Deputy, and afterwards, when disaster came thick upon disaster, he followed his patron back to London. In fear and trembling, he presented himself before the enraged Elizabeth. "What!" she cried, "did the fool bring you too?" The terrified poet fell upon his knees, while the Queen, as he afterwards described it, "chafed much, walked fastly too and fro, and looked with discomposure in her visage". Then, suddenly rushing towards him, she caught hold of his girdle. "By God's Son", she shouted, "I am no Queen, and that man is above me!" His stammering excuses were cut short with a "Go back to your business!" uttered in such a tone that Sir John, not staying to be bidden twice, fled out of the room, and fled down to Kelston, "as if all the Irish rebels had been at his heels".'

Despite the fact that Sir John was to make a brief unexplained appearance in the epilogue to *Gloriana* where his participation in the Irish expedition is specifically mentioned, Plomer ignored this intensely dramatic material.

There was also the celebrated scene in the Council Chamber, when Essex obstructed by the Queen in the matter of the Irish appointment, lost his temper and turned his back on her. Crying 'Go to the devil!' she boxed his ears, whereat he clapped his hand to his sword and shouted 'This is an outrage that I will not put up with. I would not have borne it from your father's hands.' Plomer did not use this episode either, though he allowed Essex to make a brief, though hardly noticeable, reference to it in Act II, Scene iii.

Cuffe appears in the libretto as a minor character, a feed to Essex. More extended treatment is given to Cecil, Raleigh and Mountjoy, though the result is still somewhat

perfunctory when their operatic characters are compared
with historical reality. The two women—the Countess of
Essex and Penelope, Lady Rich—emerge rather more
successfully, partly because less is actually known about
them, and the librettist has had a freer hand accordingly.
Many facets of Essex's character are shown: the proud and
tetchy nobleman; the lover and poet; the romantic
advocate of the simple life; the ambitious courtier; the
sullen conspirator; the unsuccessful general. But he disappears completely after his return from Ireland; and
although his final act of treason—his march through the
City of London and call to insurrection—is depicted indirectly in Act III, Scene ii, he himself is not shown at the
head of his followers, nor does he appear in connection
with his condemnation.

So far it would seem as if the historical picture presented by the opera is a partial and incomplete one. But
one character remains—Elizabeth herself—and as soon as
she is considered, the whole perspective of the opera
changes and everything seems to fall into focus. It is then
clear that the episode of Essex has been used only insofar as
it helps to place in relief her character as a Queen who,
though ageing, is still at the height of her powers; and it is
here that Britten and Plomer have scored their most in-
controvertible success. Even a scene like the Masque at the
Norwich Guildhall (II, i), which ostensibly has nothing to
do with the plot, is vital to the opera, since it shows that
it was an important part of the Sovereign's functions to
accept graciously the ceremonial that inevitably accompanied her progresses through her kingdom.

Elizabeth first appears (I, i) leaving a tilting ground after
a tournament. It is one of her public appearances, and she
is accompanied by a retinue and preceded by trumpeters.
Her pompous entry disturbs a brawl between Essex and
Mountjoy, whom she has just honoured for his prowess in

the tiltyard with the gift of a golden queen from her set of
chessmen. She summons her subjects to hear her judgment
and forbids Essex and Mountjoy to continue their private
quarrel. A feature of this scene is the loyal chorus:

> *Green leaves are we,*
> *Red rose our golden Queen,*
> *O crownèd rose among the leaves so green!*

The following scene (I, ii) is laid in one of her private
apartments at Nonesuch. First, she discusses public and
private business with Cecil, whose precepts on government
give something of the impression of wheels moving within
wheels. Essex arrives. Dismissing Cecil, she abandons herself to the pleasure of his company, well aware of the
weakness of his character as well as his charm. After singing two lute songs to entertain her, the second of which is a
setting of a poem '*Happy were he*' actually written by the
original Earl of Essex, he urges his claim to be sent to
Ireland to conquer the rebel Tyrone; but she easily evades
giving an answer. Left alone, she soliloquizes:

> *If life were love and love were true,*
> *Then could I love thee through and through!*
> *But God gave me a sceptre,*
> > *The burden and the glory—*
> *I must not lay them down*
> > *I live and reign a virgin,*
> > > *Will die in honour,*
> *Leave a refulgent crown!*

In the second act she is shown on two ceremonial
occasions: the first at Norwich, where she receives the
homage of the citizens and is entertained with a rustic
masque; and the second at the Palace of Whitehall, where
she enjoys an evening of dancing. These are separated by a
short scene in the garden of Essex House where Mountjoy's
secret tryst with Lady Rich is interrupted by the appear-

ance of Essex complaining to his wife of his treatment by the Queen. Lady Rich, Essex and Mountjoy discuss the possibility of seizing the reins of State, while Lady Essex counsels caution.

During the dancing at the Palace of Whitehall (II, iii), there is an episode that shows how spiteful Elizabeth could be, particularly to women who were in any way connected with men she was interested in. Noticing that Lady Essex is dressed with special magnificence, she gets hold of her dress through a stratagem and puts it on herself. It is a gross misfit, and the effect is grotesque. She parades in it before the Court to the extreme confusion of Lady Essex. In all this Plomer has kept fairly close to historical accuracy, his only major change being to transfer the affair of the dress from Lady Mary Howard, whom the Queen actually suspected of an intrigue with Essex, to Lady Essex herself. The attack on Lady Essex is so savage and wilful that when the Queen sweeps offstage, the feelings of the group of would-be conspirators (Lady Rich, Essex and Mountjoy) are roused to fury. First they seek to comfort Lady Essex—'*Good Frances, do not weep*'—and then Essex bursts out with his bitter taunt, '*Her conditions are as crooked as her carcass!*' Suddenly Elizabeth returns in state with her councillors and announces she has appointed Essex Lord Deputy in Ireland. The moment is brilliantly chosen. At a stroke Essex's heart empties of all rancour. He accepts the honour and charge, and assures his Sovereign '*With God's help I will have victory, and you shall have peace*'.

Vain words! The campaign is a calamity; Tyrone and his Irish kerns are unvanquished. Essex, seeing the extent of his failure, panics and, leaving his troops in the lurch, returns hurriedly, unannounced, to England. He breaks in on the Queen early in the morning at Nonesuch, while she is at her toilet 'in a dressing-gown, unpainted, without her wig, her grey hair hanging in wisps about her face, and her eyes

starting from her head'.[1] Surprised though she is by his
sudden irruption, not for one moment does she lose command of the situation. Essex talks of forgiveness, babbles of
foes who beset him in England, reminds her of his love—
but all to no purpose. Elizabeth knows instinctively he has
failed in her trust, and her view is confirmed by Cecil. She
makes up her mind. Essex must be kept under guard lest
he and his followers prove a danger to the realm. To Cecil
she confesses:

> *I have failed to tame my thoroughbred.*
> *He is still too proud*
> *And I must break his will*
> *And pull down his great heart.*
> *It is I who have to rule.*

Nevertheless, Essex and his followers break out in an
abortive attempt to rouse the citizens of London, the rising
goes off at half-cock, and Essex is proclaimed a traitor
(III, ii).

The final scene (III, iii) begins just after the trial, when
Essex has been found guilty and condemned to death. The
verdict is communicated to the Queen, who hesitates for
the moment to sign her favourite's death warrant. Then she
grants an audience to Lady Essex and Lady Rich, who both
beg for his life. To Lady Essex she is gracious, promising
protection for his children. Lady Rich, however, antag-
onizes her with her obstinate, insolent importuning. The
Queen sees that further delay would be fatal. Summoning
up all her fortitude, she signs the warrant.

At this point in the opera, the stage darkens, the Queen is
left alone, and there is an epilogue during which time and
place become of less and less importance. This is a passage
that is always likely to excite controversy. Whereas
Strachey ended *Queen Victoria* with a virtuoso coda in

---

[1]Lytton Strachey, *op. cit.*

which he drew together many of the varied strands of Victoria's long life in a long last flashback, in *Elizabeth and Essex* he was content with a final section depicting the gradual stages of Elizabeth's final dissolution. This has been used by Britten and Plomer as basis for a pre-view of six brief episodes that were to occur after Essex's beheading and before Elizabeth's death. A fully orchestrated version of Essex's second lute-song '*Happy were he*' accompanies these episodes, in some of which new, hitherto unintroduced characters (such as Sir John Harington) appear. Many of the words in this epilogue are based on actually recorded speech. Only three phrases are actually sung by Elizabeth, two of them echoes of Essex's lute-song:

> *In some unhaunted desert . . .*
> *There might he sleep secure . . .*
> *Mortua, mortua, sed non sepulta . . .*

Otherwise, the dialogue is melodramatic, the music being interrupted to admit speech over sustained tremolo strings, wind, or percussion. The procedure may be unorthodox, but it is undeniably effective in the theatre. Nearly all the words—particularly Elizabeth's speech to the audience, which is derived from her Golden Speech to Parliament—are given maximum clarity; and the lute-song itself rings out nobly in its full orchestral apotheosis, cracked though it be by the six melodramatic interruptions.

The whole opera ends with an off-stage repeat of the chorus '*Green leaves are we*' that dies away into silence.

II

Gloriana is the only thorough-composed opera of Britten's in which the acts are not unbroken musical entities. Each of the eight scenes, which make up the opera's three acts, is complete in itself and has attached to it a brief orchestral prelude that is played before the curtain rises.

The result is that, while the opera lacks the cumulative musical flow of *Peter Grimes*, or *The Rape of Lucretia*, or *Billy Budd*, it provides a succession of vivid self-contained tableaux.

The prelude to Act I, Scene i, which is more extended than any of the others, repeats the device originally used in the storm interlude of *Peter Grimes*. It gives a graphic musical description of the jousting in the lists, with each charge introduced by a lively sennet on the brass; and when the curtain rises, the same music is repeated quietly to accompany Cuffe's running description of the tournament that is taking place offstage. After the victor (Mountjoy) has been presented with a golden prize by the Queen, the crowd turns to her and acclaims her in a solemn hymn.

Ex. 65

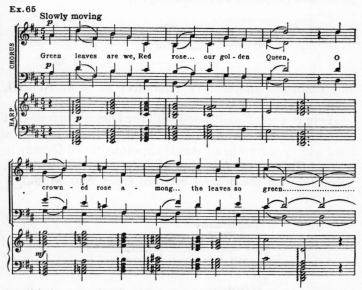

This is one of Britten's most genial inventions. Its slowly moving intervals, especially the 6ths, 7ths and 9ths, unfold

like the petals of a multifoliate Tudor rose, and the sensation that they overlap each other is enhanced by the 5/4
time signature. The chorus is repeated in Act II, Scene i
and Act III, Scene iii; and it is not surprising to find it
associated in other ways with the course of the opera. It has
already been used as the bass for one of the clanking
episodes in the jousting prelude to Act I, Scene i:

it provides an introductory flourish for the different
phrases of Elizabeth's soliloquy (I, ii):

and there are momentary references to it in Act III,
Scenes i and iii.

There is a motif associated with the Queen's favour that
deserves special attention. It is based on the notes of the
triad and appears when Essex is appointed Lord Deputy in
Ireland (Ex: 68 (*a*)), having already occurred in Act I,
Scene i during the quarrel between Essex and Mountjoy
(Ex: 68 (*b*)):

With an altered coda, it forms the theme of the trio (II, iii)
'*Good Frances, do not weep*' (Ex: 69 (*a*)) and also of Lady
Rich's pleading for Essex's life (III, iii), which so exasperates
the Queen by its obstinate persistence (Ex: 69 (*b*)):

There are moments when this fanfare-like theme reminds
one of some of the oracular passages in Strawinsky's
Oedipus Rex.

Much of the score is sparse and muscular; and there is
no flabby harmonization just for the sake of filling-in.
Sometimes monody is sufficient for Britten's purpose, as is
the case with the first part of the unaccompanied song of
the Country Girls in the Masque (II, i) '*Sweet flag and
cuckoo flower*' with its characteristic Lydian fourth, and the
flute solo accompanied by a tabor for the Morris Dance
(II, ii) which recalls the earlier *Metamorphoses after Ovid*.

At the same time there are finely constructed passages
such as the Ensemble of Reconciliation (I, i), the whole

sequence of intimate lyrical ensembles in Act II, Scene ii
(duet, double duet, and quartet), and the particularly
beautiful Dressing-Table Song (III, i) sung by the Lady in
Waiting with a chorus of Maids of Honour.

And a special word of praise should go to the dances in
Act II, Scene iii. Here the succession of Pavane, Galliard,
Lavolta, March and Coranto succeeds in capturing the
genuine Elizabethan idiom with its cross-rhythms, false
relations, crazy filigree ornamentation and heavy bounding
basses.

There are many felicitous touches of musical characterization. For instance, although the Recorder of Norwich
has only eight bars in Act II, Scene i, he is so firmly drawn
that he remains as vividly in one's memory as if he had
been a character in Crabbe's *The Borough*.

But ultimately it is through the imaginative presentation
of the Queen who gave her name to the age and was its
chief ornament and glory that the opera triumphs.

APPENDICES

APPENDIX A

Chronological List of Works

Note: All Britten's works are published by Boosey & Hawkes, with the exception of those marked with an asterisk, which are published by the Oxford University Press, and the one marked with a dagger, which is published by A. & C. Black Ltd., The Year Book Press. *Paul Bunyan* and *An Occasional Overture in C*, though performed, have not been published. Britten's incidental music for the theatre, radio, cinema and ballet is not included—nor are his Purcell realizations.

1929

THE BIRDS: song for voice and piano (words by Hilaire Belloc)—revised in 1934

1930

HYMN TO THE VIRGIN: anthem for mixed voices unaccompanied (words anon.)—revised in 1934

1932

*THREE TWO-PART SONGS: for boys' or female voices and piano (words by Walter de la Mare)—1. The Ride-by-Nights; 2. The Rainbow; 3. The Ship of Rio

SINFONIETTA: for chamber orchestra, op. 1

PHANTASY QUARTET: for oboe, violin, viola and cello, op. 2

1933

*A BOY WAS BORN: choral variations for mixed voices unaccompanied, op. 3 (words selected from *Ancient English Christmas Carols* and the *Oxford Book of Carols*)

TWO PART SONGS: for mixed voices and piano—1. I Lov'd a Lass (words by George Wither); 2. Lift Boy (words by Robert Graves)

1934

*SIMPLE SYMPHONY: for string orchestra or string quartet, op. 4

HOLIDAY DIARY: suite for piano, op. 5

FRIDAY AFTERNOONS: twelve songs (two volumes) for children's voices and piano, op. 7 (words selected from *Tom Tiddler's Ground* by Walter de la Mare and from other sources)

†MAY: unison song with piano

1935

*TE DEUM IN C MAJOR: for choir and organ

SUITE: for violin and piano, op. 6

1936

OUR HUNTING FATHERS: symphonic cycle for high voice and orchestra, op. 8 (words by W. H. Auden)

SOIREES MUSICALES: suite of five movements from Rossini for orchestra, op. 9

1937

VARIATIONS ON A THEME OF FRANK BRIDGE: for string orchestra, op. 10

ON THIS ISLAND: five songs for high voice and piano, op. 11 (words by W. H. Auden)

TWO BALLADS: for two sopranos and piano—1. Mother Comfort (words by Montagu Slater); 2. Underneath the Abject Willow (words by W. H. Auden)

FISH IN THE UNRUFFLED LAKES: song for voice and piano (words by W. H. Auden)

MONT JUIC: suite of Catalan Dances for orchestra, op. 12—written with Lennox Berkeley

1938

PIANO CONCERTO No. 1 in D, op. 13—revised in 1946

ADVANCE DEMOCRACY: chorus for mixed voices unaccompanied (words by Randall Swingler)

1939

BALLAD OF HEROES: for high voice, chorus and orchestra, op. 14 (words by W. H. Auden and Randall Swingler)

VIOLIN CONCERTO No. 1, op. 15—revised in 1950

CANADIAN CARNIVAL (KERMESSE CANADIENNE): for orchestra, op. 19

LES ILLUMINATIONS: for high voice and string orchestra, op. 18 (words by Arthur Rimbaud)

1940

SINFONIA DA REQUIEM: for orchestra, op. 20

DIVERSIONS ON A THEME: for piano (left hand) and orchestra, op. 21—revised in 1950

SEVEN SONNETS OF MICHELANGELO: for tenor and piano, op. 22

1941

PAUL BUNYAN: operetta (libretto by W. H. Auden)

MATINEES MUSICALES: second suite of five movements from Rossini for orchestra, op. 24

INTRODUCTION AND RONDO ALLA BURLESCA: for two pianos, op. 23 No. 1

MAZURKA ELEGIACA: for two pianos, op. 23 No. 2

SCOTTISH BALLAD: for two pianos and orchestra, op. 26

STRING QUARTET No. 1 in D, op. 25

1942

HYMN TO ST. CECILIA: for mixed voices unaccompanied, op. 27 (words by W. H. Auden)

A CEREMONY OF CAROLS: for treble voices and harp, op. 28 (words by James, John and Robert Wedderburn, Robert Southwell, William Cornish, and from anonymous sources)

FOLK SONG ARRANGEMENTS: for voice and piano (Vol. I British Isles)—1. The Sally Gardens; 2. Little Sir William; 3. The Bonny Earl o' Moray; 4. O Can Ye Sew Cushions?; 5. The Trees They Grow so High; 6. The Ash Grove; 7. Oliver Cromwell

1943

PRELUDE AND FUGUE: for eighteen-part string orchestra, op. 29

REJOICE IN THE LAMB: festival cantata for choir and organ, op. 30 (words by Christopher Smart)

SERENADE: for tenor, horn and strings, op. 31 (words by Cotton, Tennyson, Blake, anon., Ben Jonson and Keats)

THE BALLAD OF LITTLE MUSGRAVE AND LADY BARNARD: for male voices and piano (words anon.)

1945

PETER GRIMES: opera, op. 33 (libretto by Montagu Slater)

FESTIVAL TE DEUM: for choir and organ, op. 32

THE HOLY SONNETS OF JOHN DONNE: for tenor and piano, op. 35 op. 35

STRING QUARTET No. 2 in C, op. 36

1946

THE RAPE OF LUCRETIA: opera, op. 37 (libretto by Ronald Duncan) —revised in 1947

AN OCCASIONAL OVERTURE IN C: for orchestra, op. 38

FOLK SONG ARRANGEMENTS: for voice and piano (Vol. II France) —1. La Noël passée; 2. Voici le Printemps; 3. Fileuse; 4. Le roi s'en va-t'en chasse; 5. La Belle est au jardin d'amour; 6. Il est quelqu'un sur terre; 7 Eho! Eho!; 8. Quand j'étais chez mon père

THE YOUNG PERSON'S GUIDE TO THE ORCHESTRA: variations and fugue on a theme by Purcell, op. 34

1947

ALBERT HERRING: comic opera, op. 39 (libretto by Eric Crozier)

PRELUDE AND FUGUE ON A THEME OF VITTORIA : for organ

CANTICLE I: for tenor and piano, op. 40 (words by Francis Quarles)

A CHARM OF LULLABIES: for mezzo-soprano and piano, op. 41 (words by Blake, Burns, Robert Greene, Thomas Randolph and John Philip)

1948

FOLK SONG ARRANGEMENTS: for voice and piano (Vol. III British Isles)—1. The Plough Boy; 2. There's None to Soothe; 3. Sweet Polly Oliver; 4. The Miller of Dee; 5. The Foggy, Foggy Dew; 6. O Waly, Waly; 7. Come you not from Newcastle?

SAINT NICOLAS: cantata for tenor, mixed voices, string orchestra, piano, percussion and organ, op. 42 (words by Eric Crozier)

THE BEGGAR'S OPERA: a new realization of John Gay's ballad opera, op. 43

1949

SPRING SYMPHONY: for soprano, alto and tenor soli, mixed chorus, boys' choir and orchestra, op. 44 (words from various sources)

THE LITTLE SWEEP: opera for young people, op. 45 (libretto by Eric Crozier)

A WEDDING ANTHEM (Amo Ergo Sum): for soprano and tenor soli, choir and organ, op. 46 (words by Ronald Duncan)

1950

FIVE FLOWER SONGS: for unaccompanied mixed chorus, op. 47—1. To Daffodils (words by Robert Herrick); 2. The Succession of the Four Sweet Months (Robert Herrick); 3. Marsh Flowers (George Crabbe); 4. The Evening Primrose (John Clare); 5. Ballad of Green Broom (anon.)

LACHRYMÆ—Reflections on a Song of Dowland: for viola and piano, op. 48

1951

SIX METAMORPHOSES AFTER OVID: for oboe solo, op. 49—1. Pan; 2. Phaeton; 3. Niobe; 4. Bacchus; 5. Narcissus; 6. Arethusa

BILLY BUDD: opera, op. 50 (libretto by E. M. Forster and Eric Crozier)

1952

CANTICLE II—Abraham and Isaac: for alto, tenor and piano, op. 51 (text from the Chester Miracle Play)

1953

GLORIANA: opera, op. 53 (libretto by William Plomer)

WINTER WORDS: for tenor and piano, op. 52 (lyrics and ballads by Thomas Hardy)

APPENDIX B
List of Opera Productions

The entries in this appendix are set out in the same way as those in Alfred Loewenberg's *Annals of Opera:* 1597–1940. Details of first productions are followed by details of subsequent productions; but only the date of the first performance of any particular production is given, except where a production is toured. Abbreviations are used for certain theatres, as follows:

Berlin, O = *Staatsoper*   Milan, Sc. = *(Teatro alla) Scala*
Brussels, M = *(Théâtre de la)*   New York, M = *Metropolitan*
             Monnaie   Paris, O = *Opéra*
London, C.G. = *Covent Garden*   Rome, T. R. = *Teatro Reale*
          S.W. = *Sadler's Wells*   Vienna, O = *Staatsoper*
                              F = *festival*

Broadcast performances are included only when they have preceded actual stage performances. No broadcasts of live performances are mentioned. A special point has been made of listing the towns visited by companies on tour. In the case of Britten this is particularly important in view of the extensive tours of the English Opera Group, and also of companies such as the one specially promoted by the Arts Council of Australia (N.S.W. Division) to tour *Let's Make an Opera!*

PAUL BUNYAN
5.v.1941   NEW YORK, BRANDER MATTHEWS HALL

Text by W. H. Auden. *Operetta.* Prologue and two acts. Britten's first operatic venture.

PETER GRIMES
7.vi.1945   LONDON, S.W.

Text by Montagu Slater (founded on the poem by George Crabbe). Prologue and three acts.

Stockholm	21.iii.1946	
Basle	6.v.1946	(in German, transl. by Herbert Herlitschka)
Antwerp	25.v.1946	(in Flemish)
Zurich	1.vi.1946	(in German)
Tanglewood, Lenox, Mass.	6.viii.1946	(Berkshire Music Center)

Rome	7.xii.1946	(Radio Italiana broadcast)
Prague	1947	(radio broadcast)
Mannheim	1947	(in German)
Sydney, N.S.W. Conservatorium	8.iii.1947	(concert performance broadcast)
Milan, Sc.	11.iii.1947	(in Italian, transl. by M. Mila)
Hamburg	22.iii.1947	(in German)
Berlin	23.v.1947	
Brno	28.vi.1947	
Graz	9.vii.1947	
Copenhagen	15.ix.1947	
London, C.G.	6.xi.1947	

Covent Garden Opera Company on tour:

Brussels, M	7.vi.1948
Paris, O	9.vi.1948
Liverpool	7.iii.1949
Manchester	21.iv.1949
Leeds	8.iv.1949
Birmingham	11.iv.1949
Wiesbaden (F)	v.1954

| Budapest | 20.xii.1947 | |
| New York, M | 12.ii.1948 | (in English) |

Metropolitan Opera Company on tour:

Philadelphia	17.ii.1948
Boston	31.iii.1949
Los Angeles	3.v.1949

| Stanford, California | 26.v.1948 | (Stanford University Opera Workshop) |

Stanford University Opera Workshop on tour:

Los Angeles	29.vi.1948	
Oldenburg	vi.1948	(in German)
Helsinki	17.iii.1949	
Strasbourg	24.iii.1949	(in French, transl. by Roger Lalande)
Schwerin	xii.1951	(in German)
Ravag	1952	(broadcast in German)
Toronto, Canada	27.ii.1952	(Canadian Broadcasting Corporation broadcast)
Boston, Mass.	30.v.1953	(New England Conservatory of Music—excerpts only)
Brussels, M	29.i.1954	(in French)

THE RAPE OF LUCRETIA

12.vii.1946   GLYNDEBOURNE OPERA HOUSE, SUSSEX

Text by Ronald Duncan (after *Le Viol de Lucrèce* by André Obey). Two acts. Britten's first chamber opera.

Glyndebourne Productions Ltd. on tour:

Manchester	29.vii.1946
Liverpool	5.viii.1946
Edinburgh	12.viii.1946
Glasgow	19.viii.1946
London, S.W.	26.viii.1946
Oxford	23.ix.1946
Amsterdam	2.x.1946
The Hague	6.x.1946

English Opera Group on tour:

Glyndebourne	7.vii.1947
Scheveningen (F)	24.vii.1947
Amsterdam (F)	29.vii.1947
Lucerne (F)	12.viii.1947
Newcastle upon Tyne	1.x.1947
London, C.G.	10.x.1947
(100th performance, 17.x.47)	
Bournemouth	21.x.1947
Oxford	28.x.1947
Aldeburgh (F)	10.vi.1949
Wolverhampton	29.vi.1949
Cheltenham (F)	6.vii.1949
Copenhagen	12.ix.1949
Oslo	21.ix.1949
London, Lyric Theatre, Hammersmith (F)	11.v.1951
Wiesbaden (F)	31.v.1951
Schwetzingen (F)	v.1954
York (F)	28.vi.1954

Brussels, M	25.iv.1947	
Chicago	1.vi.1947	
Basle	5.vi.1947	(in German, transl. by Elisabeth Mayer)
Hollywood	17.vi.1947	(Hollywood Chamber Opera)

Sydney, N.S.W.	25.x.1947	(concert performance)
St. Louis, Missouri	3.iv.1948	(St. Louis Grand Opera Guild)
Mulhouse	4.iv.1948	(in French, transl. Georges Dalman)

Mulhouse Municipal Theatre Opera Company on tour:

Paris	19.v.1948	
Colmar	7.iv.1948	
Stockholm	7.v.1948	(radio broadcast)
Strasbourg	23.x.1948	(in French)
Cologne	9.xi.1948	(in German)
New York	30.xii.1948	(twenty-three performances)
Rome, T.R.	12.ii.1949	(in Italian, transl. by M. Mucci)
Lübeck	17.x.1949	(in German)
Gothenburg	17.x.1949	

Stora Teatern Gothenburg Opera Company on tour:

Stockholm	2.xi.1949	
Stuttgart	i.1950	(Süddeutscher Rundfunk broadcast)
Seattle, Washington	18.v.1950	(University of Washington)
Munich	vi.1950	(Bayerischer Rundfunk broadcast)
Bremen	viii.1950	(Radio Bremen broadcast)
Salzburg (F)	9.viii.1950	(in German)
Aachen	xi.1950	(in German)
Kassel	8.xi.1950	(in German)
Morocco	20.ii.1951	(Radio Maroc broadcast)
Darmstadt	17.iv.1951	(in German)
Pittsburgh, Pennsylvania	27.vii.1951	(Pennsylvania College for Women)
Munich, Bayerischer Staatsoper	24.xi.1951	(in German)
New York	13.ii.1952	(Opera Futures Workshop)
Tunis	8.viii.1952	(Radio Tunis broadcast)
Antwerp	22.xi.1952	(in Flemish)
Hamburg	22.i.1953	(in German)
Cleveland, Ohio	2.v.1953	
Wiesbaden	7.ix.1953	(in German)
Münster	8.xi.1953	(in German)
Stuttgart	20.ii.1954	(in German)

ALBERT HERRING

20.vi.1947   GLYNDEBOURNE OPERA HOUSE, SUSSEX

Text by Eric Crozier (after *Le Rosier de Madame Husson* by Guy de Maupassant). *Comic Opera*. Three acts. Britten's second chamber opera.

English Opera Group on tour:

Scheveningen (F)	22.vii.1947
Lucerne (F)	15.viii.1947
Newcastle-upon-Tyne	29.ix.1947
London, C.G.	8.x.1947
Bournemouth	20.x.1947
Oxford	27.x.1947
Aldeburgh (F)	7.vi.1948
Cheltenham (F)	7.vii.1948
Cambridge	26.vii.1948
London, S.W.	8.ix.1948
Birmingham	29.ix.1948
London, People's Palace	13.x.1948
Aldeburgh (F)	15.vi.1949
Wolverhampton	27.vi.1949
Cheltenham (F)	4.vii.1949
Copenhagen	13.ix.1949
Oslo	19.ix.1949
London, Lyric Theatre, Hammersmith (F)	2.v.1951
Aldeburgh (F)	11.vi.1951
Liverpool (F)	1.viii.1951
Wiesbaden (F)	10.v.1953
Aldeburgh (F)	20.vi.1953

Brussels, M	1.vi.1948	
Tanglewood, Lenox, Mass.	8.viii.1949	(Berkshire Music Center)
Los Angeles	xi.1949	(University of Southern California)
Boston, Mass.	15.i.1950	(New England Opera Theatre)
Cincinnati, Ohio	21.iv.1950	(Cincinnati Music Drama Guild)
Hanover	11.vi.1950	(in German, transl. by Fritz Schröder)
Denver, Colorado	17.viii.1950	(University of Denver)
London, R.A.M.	ix.1950	
Berlin, Städtische Oper	3.xi.1950	(in German)
Antwerp	16.xii.1950	(in Flemish)
Brunswick	29.v.1951	(in German)

Toronto, Canada	10.i.1951	(Canadian Broadcasting Corporation broadcast)
Morocco	20.ii.1951	(Radio Maroc broadcast)
Gothenburg Stora Teatern	9.iv.1951	
Lübeck	4.vi.1951	(in German)
Baltimore, Maryland	3.xi.1951	(Baltimore Chamber Music Society)
Freiburg	vi.1952	(in German)
New York	2.vi.1952	(Opera Futures)
Evanston, Illinois	30.i.1953	(Northwestern University)
Copenhagen	1953	

Copenhagen Opera Company on tour:

Flensburg		
Schleswig		
Frankfurt	9.v.1953	(Hessischer Rundfunk broadcast)
Munich	29.v.1953	(Rundfunk broadcast)
Stuttgart	27.xii.1953	(Süddeutscher Rundfunk broadcast)

THE BEGGAR'S OPERA (1728)

24.v.1948   CAMBRIDGE ARTS THEATRE

A new musical version of John Gay's ballad opera. Three acts. Written as a chamber opera.

English Opera Group on tour:

Amsterdam (F)	25.vi.1948
Utrecht (F)	26.vi.1948
Rotterdam (F)	29.vi.1948
Scheveningen (F)	30.vi.1948
Cheltenham (F)	5.vii.1948
Knokke (F)	21.vii.1948
London, S.W.	6.ix.1948
Birmingham	27.ix.1948
London, People's Palace	11.x.1948
Aldeburgh (F)	19.vi.1950
Cheltenham (F)	11.vii.1950
London, Lyric Theatre, Hammersmith	17.vii.1950
Barnstaple (F)	14.vii.1953

New York	24.iii.1949	(Juilliard School of Music)
Vienna, O	7.i.1950	(in German)
Basle	5.ii.1950	(in German)
Philadelphia, Penn.	2.iii.1950	(Chamber Opera Society)

Lucerne	26.iii.1950	
Los Angeles	24.v.1950	(University of California)
Hamburg	23.vi.1950	(in German)
Wiesbaden	28.i.1951	(in German)
Berlin (F)	18.ix.1951	(in German)
Innsbruck	6.ii.1952	(in German)
Amherst, Mass.	19.ii.1953	(Amherst College)
Cincinnati, Ohio	5.v.1953	(Cincinnati Music-Drama Guild)
Krefeld	1953	

THE LITTLE SWEEP

14.vi.1949   ALDEBURGH, JUBILEE HALL (F)

Text by Eric Crozier. One act. The opera from *Let's Make an Opera!* an entertainment for young people.

English Opera Group on tour:

Wolverhampton	28.vi.1949
Cheltenham (F)	5.vii.1949
Aldeburgh	22.viii.1949
Cambridge	31.x.1949
Brighton	7.xi.1949
London, Lyric Theatre, Hammersmith	15.xi.1949
Aldeburgh (F)	20.vi.1950
Cheltenham (F)	15.vii.1950
Tunbridge Wells	28.ix.1950
Eastbourne	2.x.1950
Brighton	6.xi.1950
Torquay	13.xi.1950
Cambridge	20.xi.1950
Birmingham	27.xi.1950
London, Lyric Theatre, Hammersmith	4.xii.1950
London, Lyric Theatre, Hammersmith (F)	5.v.1951
Lowestoft	4.vi.1951
Liverpool (F)	2.viii.1951
London, Lyric Theatre, Hammersmith	24.xii.1951
Hull	25.ii.1952
Wimbledon	17.iii.1952
Barnstaple (F)	16.vii.1953

Saint Louis, Miss.	22.iii.1950	(Music Educators' National Conference)
Boulder, Colorado	18.v.1950	(University of Colorado)
Seattle, Washington	9.vi.1950	(Seattle Repertory Playhouse)
Lisbon, New Hampshire	22.viii.1950	(Camp Ogontz)
Nürnberg-Furth	ix.1950	
Oslo	12.x.1950	
Cleveland, Ohio	18.x.1950	(Karamu Opera House)
Zurich	30.x.1950	(in German, transl. by Bettina Hürlimann)
Boston, New York	20.xi.1950	(Show of the Month Club)
Gelsenkirchen	10.i.1951	
Philadelphia, Penn.	12.iii.1951	(Board of Education—Academy of Vocal Arts)
Nürnberg	7.iv.1951	
Geneva, Conservatoire de Musique	iv.1951	(French transl. by Samuel Baud Bovy)
Boston, Mass.	5.v.1951	(Zimbler String Sinfonietta)
Los Angeles, California	26.v.1951	
Oldenburg	16.vi.1951	
Tübingen	24.vii.1951	(Opernstudio)
Detmold	vii.1951	(Mus. Akademie)
Sydney, N.S.W. Palace Theatre	7.ix.1951	
Canberra, Albert Hall	8.x.1951	
Brisbane, His Majesty's Theatre	15.x.1951	

The Arts Council of Australia (*N.S.W. Division*) *production on tour :*

Wollongong	18.ii.1952	Wagga	10.iii.1952
Bowral	20.ii.1952	Leeton	13.iii.1952
Moss Vale	21.ii.1952	Griffith	14.iii.1952
Crookwell	25.ii.1952	Condobolin	18.iii.1952
Goulburn	26.ii.1952	Parkes	19.iii.1952
Yass	28.ii.1952	Dubbo	21.iii.1952
Young	3.iii.1952	Orange	24.iii.1952
Cootamundra	4.iii.1952	Cowra	25.iii.1952
Temora	5.iii.1952	Bathurst	26.iii.1952
Junee	6.iii.1952	Lithgow	28.iii.1952

Maitland	31.iii.1952	Moree	7.vii.1952
Kurri Kurri	1.iv.1952	Warialda	8.vii.1952
Cessnock	2.iv.1952	Inverell	9.vii.1952
Singleton	4.iv.1952	Armidale	10.vii.1952
Newcastle	7.iv.1952	Tenterfield	14.vii.1952
Muswellbrook	30.vi.1952	Lismore	16.vii.1952
Tamworth	1.vii.1952	Grafton	17.vii.1952
Gunnedah	3.vii.1952	Kempsey	21.vii.1952
Narrabri	4.vii.1952	Taree	23.vii.1952

The total attendances at the eighty-seven performances on this tour were: children 34,100, adults 9,960—total 44,060.

Antwerp, Volba	6.xi.1951	
Louisville, Kentucky	7.xii.1951	(WHAS, Inc.)
Luxembourg	29.iii.1952	(Radio Luxembourg)
Remsheid	17.v.1952	
Lüdenscheid	21.v.1952	
Heidelberg	8.vi.1952	(Junge Opernbühne)
Berlin, Tribüne	29.vi.1952	
Ulm	21.ix.1952	
Tel Aviv, Israel	ix.1952	(in Hebrew, transl. by Mordecai Tel-Zur)
Antwerp	2.x.1952	
Rotterdam	13.x.1952	
Oregon	14.xi.1952	(Oregon Music Educators Assoc.)
St. Louis, Missouri	5.iii.1953	(Central Opera Association)
Manila, Philippine Is.	16.iii.1953	(Philippine Women's University)
Tallahassee, Florida	22.iv.1953	(Florida State University)
Hamburg	1953	
Hagen	10.vi.1953	
Baden Baden	2.x.1953	(Südwestfunk broadcast)
Basle, Comödie	1954	(in Baseldytsch, transl. by Otto Müller)
Hanover	1953	

DIDO AND AENEAS (1689)

1.v.1951   LONDON, LYRIC, HAMMERSMITH (F)

Text by Nahum Tate. Opera in three acts by Henry Purcell, in a new realization by Benjamin Britten.

English Opera Group on tour:
Aldeburgh (F)   8.vi.1951

Amsterdam (F)	20.vi.1951
The Hague (F)	21.vi.1951
Cheltenham (F)	10.vii.1951
Liverpool (F)	30.vii.1951

BILLY BUDD

1.xii.1951   LONDON, C.G.

Text by E. M. Forster and Eric Crozier (founded on the story by
Herman Melville). Prologue, Four Acts and Epilogue.

Covent Garden Opera Company on tour:

Cardiff	7.iii.1952
Manchester	14.iii.1952
Glasgow	28.iii.1952
Birmingham	4.iv.1952
Paris, Th. des	
Champs-Elysées (F)	26.v.1952

Wiesbaden,		(in German, transl. by Alfred H.
Staatstheater	2.iii.1952	Unger)
New York	19.xi.1952	(N.B.C.—TV Opera Workshop)
Indiana	7.xii.1952	(Indiana University)

GLORIANA

8.vi.1953   LONDON, C.G.

Text by William Plomer. Three Acts. Composed in honour of the
Coronation of H.M. Queen Elizabeth II and first given at a gala
performance in the presence of H.M. the Queen.

Covent Garden Opera Company on tour:

Bulawayo	8.viii.1953
Cardiff	11.iii.1954
Manchester	30.iii.1954
Birmingham	13.iv.1954

INDEX

Note: Theatres and opera houses in London are indexed under the general heading 'London Theatres and Opera Houses'.

Printed by
Fredk. W. Kahn Ltd., London, E.C.1